*Whatever you sell, the ch*
*to create a profitable pro* *dut delivers*
*predictable levels of new and repeat business*

# ABOUT THE AUTHORS

# David Amor

David is an award winning direct marketer and whilst working with Grey technologies he secured a first ever DMA award for a mailing house in 2014.

David has worked in the direct mail and print industries for close to three decades. Over the last 17 years, David has built his company First Move, to be a premier supplier of direct mail services, as well as a leader in associated outsourced fulfilment.

Offering a full service to its clients through proven planning and account management skills, last year First Move worked with 317 clients to mail 75 million items and despatch £1.8 million of same-day orders from its location in the Thames Valley.

Citing the valuable benefits of the DIRECT MAIL 101 programme, David's vision is to create a service that delivers better results and streamlines costs to transform businesses through direct mail.

A leading evangelist in direct mail, David continues to grow his clients' sales and generate unthought of revenue streams as he continually pioneers new direct mail practice alongside his 45 years experience of best practices.

This book is a rare insight into some, not all, of his shared knowledge.

Visit David's company website at **www.firstmove.co.uk** to find out more insights in direct mail.

# David, According To Others:

"First Move were an absolute pleasure to work with. They took the time to wholly understood our issue, and with their help aided us in unertaking a large campaign for a very blue-chip client. I would not hesitate to use them again, or indeed hesitate to recommend them to anyone. First Move? First Class in my book!"
**Boomerang Media Group**

"Just wanted to drop you a quick note to let you know that we took delivery of the catalogues today and THEY LOOK GREAT – BEAUTIFUL even  thank you so so much… You are an absolute hero for stepping in at the last minute and doing such a brilliant job, THANK YOU."
**The Great Gift Company**

"I've been using First Move for the last 3-4 years. They are always very helpful and quick to respond, and they've helped us to reduce our mailing costs.
**British Science association**

"First Move are incredibly responsive to our needs and supportive in finding solutions to our distribution requirements. First Move have helped us to save costs where possible."
**The Institute of Mechanical Engineers**

"First Move are flexible, thorough and 100% reliable, they have fast become a key member of the Lavazza UK team. Concerning our work together, they have become an integral part of the Lavazza business and are used as best practice example for all the other Lavazza countries."
**Lavazza**

# James Daniel

James is a UK copywriter
and author of the writer's
guide "Do You Talk Like
That At Home?"

Like most good copywriters,
James came late to the party
after sharpening his writing
and commercial skills in
other fields.

He spent 8 years as a journalist, then 9 years in corporate sales
and marketing - all while juggling a fistful of writing projects for
TV and radio.

By the time James trained as a copywriter at the age of 37, he
had 17 years' worth of writing credits and almost a decade at
the sharp end of corporate life - giving his clients a double-edged
insight that very few copywriters can match.

10 years on, James has worked with 200 clients in the UK,
Europe, USA and UAE. His words have sold high-end products,
business services, continuity schemes and prestige events.
In a typical year, the Royal Mail handles over 1 million copies of
James' best performing sales letters, and over 3 million copies of
his emails reach inboxes worldwide.

In 2013, James won the Canmol Technology Marketing Award
from the Chartered Institute of Marketing in Wales, recognising
a control-beating direct mail campaign created for Hidden
Hearing.

**Sign up for James' Friday email tips at www.CopyThat.Works**

# James, According To Others:

"James has a gift for writing simple, conversational copy that gently persuades. Read his work - he doesn't scream from the page, or resort to hype. He just keeps you reading and nodding along, right up until you respond."
**Jonathan Jay – CEO, The Marketing Guild**

"James' copy out-performed the letters we'd been using for years. Since then I haven't looked back…I couldn't have done it without him!"
**Lynda Dobbie – Direct Marketing Manager, Hidden Hearing**

"James is professional, keeps his word and is one of the most honourable chaps I've worked with. His attention to detail is superb, he gets direct response marketing and you won't find anyone better."
**Dave Dean – Managing Director, Riskmonitor**

"Unlike most copywriters (and I mean most!), James has a firm handle on marketing and stays permanently 'in the loop' of relevant trends, innovation and competitor activity affecting his clients' success. So his clients get more than a copywriter - they get a consultant who writes copy."
**Dr. Geraint Evans, Marketing Consultant**

And finally…last but not least: **"Your stuff is bloody good!"**
**Short & Sweet Words from Copywriting Legend Drayton Bird**

# Contents

## Foreword

## Creating The List

## Planning the Campaign

## Creating Your Offer

## Planning The Message

## Grabbing Attention with Headlines

## Winning Them Over

## Closing The Deal

## A Matter of Style

## The Package

# The Final Appraisal

# Testing & Measuring

# Appendix

# Foreword
## Do We Need Direct Mail in the 21st Century?

**Is Direct Mail old fashioned? Tired – past its Prime? Overtaken by e-mail? Too expensive to turn a profit?**

There are many business owners and even marketers who won't consider Direct Mail (DM) because in their eyes it's "expensive" and "outdated". This is a limiting belief that can handicap any business, big or small.

Since you're taking the trouble to read this, you probably see the benefits of DM. If not, then at the very least, we hope you'll approach the subject with an open mind.

By the end of this book, we hope you'll see that DM is alive and kicking – both as a source of instant profits and long-term business growth. By following the steps we've outlined, even your first campaign should deliver a good number of leads or sales. Then eventually, once you've established your "control" version, DM

14

should become a predictable – and highly profitable – marketing system.

That's not to say, of course, that you should be monogamous! In marketing, there's no silver bullet, no single marketing channel to replace all others. Success comes from testing multiple ways to communicate and sell your wares. In fact, research has shown that when a DM campaign combines with at least one other channel, results will improve by an average of 24%. Variety is the key, because everyone has their own preferred way to receive information.

Direct Mail just happens to be one of the most effective.

## So why the Recent Decline?

You may well ask, why does DM have so many detractors? If it's so effective, why are so many people reluctant to use it?

There are two main reasons.

The first is, people simply leap to the conclusion that no-one reads it. The phrase "I just throw it straight in the bin" is a stalwart of marketing meetings, but misses the point entirely. You don't need everyone to read it – just the people who are

interested! Find enough of those to turn a
profit, and it doesn't matter one bit if
everyone else throws it away. What's more,
with careful profiling, you can easily
minimise wastage.

Then, in our digital age, the second reason
for dissent is e-mail, which is undeniably
powerful - but not an alternative medium.
DM and e-mail have their own separate
virtues, and the smart marketer would never
use one to the exclusion of the other.

Let's look at their relative merits:

## The Case for E-mail

E-mail is fast and free! It's easy to plan,
schedule and deliver, and your only cost is
time. And research shows that people prefer
it as a method of communication, just as
long as they know the company that's behind
it.

But there's the rub. We all treat our
inboxes as an extension of our personal
space, and we don't like people invading it
with unsolicited messages. Sending spam -
no matter how well you've profiled your
list - can harm your reputation and create
problems with your e-mail provider. One
complaint too many, and your account will
be suspended - and that will stop your e-

mails getting through to the people who actually want them.

For now though, let's assume that your e-mails are delivered. Still, the stats show that we all treat spam with nothing but disdain. Across the board in 2013, average open rates were 19.6%. Once opened, the average click through rate was 16.9% – meaning that just 3.0% of targets actually visited a web page. That generated an average response rate of 0.12%, so (on average) you'd burn through close to 1000 prospects in order to get a sale.

That's not the full story. The survey covered a mix of campaign types – some that e-mailed with the targets' permission and some that mailed without. Not surprisingly, permission-based e-mails fared much better, with open rates peaking at 38.6%. Meaning that non-permission e-mails should expect a response rate that's significantly below average. Realistically, with a cold list, a typical business would need around 2000 addresses to generate the first sale.

These figures are only generic*, but still instructive. Clearly, e-mail can and does work, when you mail with the user's permission. There's huge value in building a list of people who want to receive your e-mails, then e-mailing regularly with a mix of offers and useful information. But e-mailing without permission puts you on a hiding to nothing. It becomes a lot of work for very little reward, with the risk of doing untold damage to your brand.

## The Case for DM

Direct Mail is a different matter entirely.

Firstly, there's little or no risk of negative association. While we resist unsolicited e-mails, we readily accept that marketing materials will arrive by post. Those who don't like it can opt out and never be troubled by DM.

Add to that the quality of consumer and business mailing lists (that let you segment by demographics, interests, affluence and buying history) and suddenly DM becomes a solid proposition. Each time you mail out, you can address the reader's personal needs with pinpoint accuracy. Plus, your reputation won't suffer, and you won't be wasting money on mailing to the wrong type of prospect.

Let's look at the numbers. For any DM campaign, the delivery rate should be close to 100%, and in B2C, 66% of consumers will keep their mail for 2 weeks or more.

DM becomes especially powerful when it sends a prospect online. On average, 44% of recipients will visit a web page, leading to an average response rate of 4%. That's over 30 responses for every one that you'd get from e-mail. In a business with long-term customer value, that's more than enough to cover the added cost and generate significant future profits.

### How to Proceed?

The obvious conclusion from these numbers would be to use DM to find new customers, then sell to existing customers by e-mail. Certainly, that's a better plan than using e-mail only! But still, it discounts DM as a tool for repeat sales and up-selling. People might say they prefer e-mail from companies they know...but a stated preference for e-mail doesn't make it more responsive! The best customer campaigns use a mix of DM and e-mail.

Consider this. Researchers at Bangor University have looked at how the brain reacts to physical and virtual messages, concluding that the "real" experience gained from physical media actively installs the message in the brain. It settles deeper in the memory, generates more emotion, creating positive brand associations and a stronger buying impulse.

That holds true, whatever the relationship between buyer and seller. Physical media is simply more powerful.

But remember, you don't have to take anyone's word for this! If you're not convinced that DM is a vital part of the marketing mix, all you have to do is test it. As with all marketing, it's best to trial on a small scale first, then scale up when it works.

If you're reluctant to even test, then consider one final statistic: DM accounts for over 60% of mail delivered in the UK. It's all trackable, so senders know where every sale has come from. So if DM didn't work, you would have stopped receiving it years ago!

## Let's get started...

In this book, we'll look at 101 separate principles that can help you to shape your first campaign and improve it each time you mail out. Whether you're a first time mailer or a seasoned DM pro...whether you're mailing to new or existing customers...you'll find ideas here that will boost your response rates, reduce mailing costs and make your next campaign all the more profitable.

We'll touch on creativity, but as you'll soon discover, successful DM is rarely the product of wild, creative thinking. Rather, it's a systematic process, where one success builds on another to the point where results become predictable – even inevitable.

On that note, we'll sign off and dive into the detail.

We would wish you good luck – but if you do this methodically, you're not going to need it!

David Amor
James Daniel
**February 2016**

*All the numbers quoted here are average figures, gained from a wide range of campaigns. They're used for illustration only, to show the relative differences between DM and e-mail that seem to apply across the board, to a greater or lesser degree.

These general statistics, especially conversion rates, may or may not apply in your business. The person who promotes a £million product to a list of random names can't expect the same response rate as the person who sells a £10 product to a list of loyal customers! The only reliable measure in your case is return on investment. We'll talk about this more in the pages that follow.

---

**Sources:**
1. Silverpop 2013 E-mail Marketing Metrics Study
2. DMA Response Rates 2012
3. Royal Mail
4. Millward Brown – Using Neuroscience to Understand the Role of Direct Mail

---

**A Word on Language:**
In this book, the word 'product' is taken to mean 'product or service'. Where a gender pronoun is used, it's intended as 'male or female'. Unless specified, 'customer' means 'existing customer or prospect'.

SECTION 1:

# Creating The List

**By far the most important piece in the DM jigsaw is the mailing list. You could write the best sales letter in history, but send it to the wrong people and it's going to bomb - guaranteed. Conversely, send a badly written letter to a well-defined audience, and it will bring in a response. It will be more trickle than flood until you fix the copy, but still the sales will come in.**

So in this first section, we're going to look at ways to build a responsive list that lets you sell the right product to the right people at the right time.

Unless you're launching a brand new business, you'll find all the answers you need in your sales ledger or customer records. With careful analysis, you'll find trends that you can replicate when you need to buy new data - and you'll find opportunities, like unconverted leads and chances to sell more to existing customers.

Let's start with the quick wins...

## 1. Find prospects who slipped through the gaps

For most companies, lead management is a random process. When someone enquires, they might receive an e-mail reply or

23

get a call from a sales person. But if they don't buy, they're forgotten - the company chases new leads instead. When you consider the cost of generating the lead, that's pure insanity.

So if your business follows the norm, you'll probably have a list of unconverted leads, just hanging around. It might not be a ready-formed list. More likely it's a combination of names on post-it notes, archived e-mails, business cards and enquiry forms! But it's still a list of people who can bring you instant business - all you have to do is give them a nudge in the right direction.

 Put your lost leads into groups or segments, based on a common link. That could be a broad link, such as an interest in a certain product. But for best results, find a narrow link like a common need or objection. If your core list is made up of people who voiced 10 different objections, create 10 segments. Then you can mail each segment with a letter that addresses their concerns directly.

## 2. Find the easy pickings in your customer list

Very few businesses manage to squeeze every penny from their customers, so it's almost certain you'll have some low hanging fruit within your list. Here are some examples:

1) Abandoned Upgrades: how many customers have begun your upgrade process, then backed out? Maybe they've

clicked a link from an email and viewed a sales page inviting them to upgrade, then given up part-way through the checkout process? These customers are interested in a premium item, but still need more convincing.

For now, you should be able to identify a portion of these leads via your email server or Content Management System. Down the line, it's worth investing in specialist software like Optilead to identify and target these customers more efficiently.

2) Non-Renewals: how many customers have bought something consumable (like skincare or cleaning products), but never come back for more? You should know the window for renewal, and there will be customers on your list who should have renewed by now...so they're ready for a reminder, and maybe a special offer that introduces them to a new product range.

3) Obsolescence: occasional purchases (like washing machines or trainers) will wear out eventually, and when they do, the customer should be coming back. Again, you'll know the window, so invite them to buy again, maybe this time with a trade-in or 'scrappage' offer.

## 3. Start building a customer model

Just by following the first two steps, you can get a few easy campaigns under your belt. But eventually, if you want to expand your business, you'll need to buy in some new data.

And you can make that process easier if you spend some time now looking through your sales and customer records, to build a customer model.

To gain some meaningful insights, you'll need to select a relevant data range. That could mean going back a few months, or even a few years. A useful rule is, use all the data you have, as long as it comes from a time that mirrors today's conditions - for example, a time when you had the same product range and broad pricing as you have today.

Once you've selected a data range for analysis, you're ready for the next step.

# 4. Create a model database

The easiest way to analyse your data is to add the relevant customer records to a dedicated spreadsheet. That's an easy step if your data is held in a database format, or if you're using a software system with a 'select and export' tool. It's more of a headache if you're working with manual records, but it shouldn't cost the earth to hire someone who can move the data across in confidence.

# 5. Define your customer types

Before you start the analysis, you should be able to break your customers down into segments or customer types. At this stage, you don't need endless detail - just choose the most significant factor, whether that's age, gender, income band, geographic region, product preference or some other divider.

For now, you'll have to rely on whatever data you have in your records. Or, if you're light on detail, ask your sales people to help you define the various customer types. The key is to keep it simple - choose a label that's easy and intuitive, like "Single Women", "Cricket Fans" or "Manufacturing Companies".

Next, go back to your model database and add a 'customer type' to each customer record. Then you're ready to analyse...

## 6. Find the vital few

You've probably heard of *The Pareto Principle*, also known as The 80/20 Split or Rule of The Vital Few. It's a phenomenon identified by Italian economist Vilfredo Pareto that can worm its way into every aspect of your business:

- 80% of your sales will come from 20% of your marketing channels

- 80% of your revenue will come from 20% of your customers

- 80% of your profits will come from 20% of your products

- 80% of your results will come from 20% of your time

And so on. The numbers won't always add up to a straight 80/20 split, but the principle is universally true: a few resources and efforts will over-deliver, while the rest will barely pull their weight.

So, this step is about finding the high 20% in your records, and ignoring the low 80%.

As you drill into the numbers, here are some questions to ask.

*It's unlikely that every question here will be relevant to your business, but if you cherry-pick the ones that apply, your answers should be revealing:*

- Which customer types are most likely to buy your entry level product?

- Which customer types are most likely to buy from you more than once?

- Which customer types stay with you for the longest time?

- Which customer types are most likely to upgrade to a premium product or subscription?

- Which product is the most popular choice for new customers?

- Which product is the most profitable?

- Which product is most likely to trigger a premium upgrade or subscription?

- When is the peak season for acquiring new customers?

# 7. Find the patterns

Let's say you've answered the questions above and found your best performers. The next step is to pull your answers together and find patterns of behaviour.

Ideally, you're looking for a product that's profitable and leads to repeat business...that's popular with a loyal, high spending customer type...and that's most likely to sell in a specific season.

That would be a winning combination of elements – or a 'Perfect Cluster'.

For example, say you run a window cleaning business offering Gold-Silver-Bronze packages to business and residential customers. You might find a pattern like this:

**25% of SMEs we speak to take our trial offer, rising to 35% from September to November. Once they've signed, 60% will upgrade from Bronze to Silver within the first 3 months. After 1 year, 30% will leave but the remaining 70% will stay with us for 3 years.**

This information would give you a range of opportunities - including:

• An upsell campaign at Month 3, where you target the 40% of SME customers who are still on the Bronze package – promoting the Silver option.

- A sales campaign, where you target new SMEs, promoting the Bronze package – with more regular mailers hitting from September to November.

- A retention or loyalty campaign, to stop customers leaving at the peak times of 1 and 3 years in.

If you can't see an obvious pattern in your data, dig a little deeper. Start by looking at the customer type that gives the best long-term profit. Then look at the best product and season for that group.

**Now find the numbers in the pattern**

The next question is, how much is this *customer plus product* pattern worth to you? And to answer that, you need to add in some hard numbers.

So, take one of your opportunities – say a sales campaign for new customers – and note the following trends:

- **Frequency:** how often will the customer buy?

- **Value:** how much will they spend each time?

- **Lifespan:** how long will they stay with you?

It doesn't matter that some customers will stay longer than others, or buy more often, or spend more. All you need is the average.

But remember, you're only analysing data from your chosen cluster. Don't skew the figures by factoring in other customer types or products.

 The numbers you get from this exercise will be a reflection of your past marketing efforts. If you're planning improvements in future, like a new upsell or retention campaign, you can expect to better your previous results. In that case, it's fine to build in some discretion, like a 10% uplift.

# 8. Calculate your average customer lifetime value

You've found the numbers, so now let's put them to work. Say you know that on average, customers will stay with you for 4 years, buy 5 times every year and spend £50 each time...then you can say with confidence that a new customer who fits the same profile should have a lifetime value of £1000 (4 x 5 x 50).

This exercise is easy if the customer type buys one single product, and buys it regularly. It's less straight forward if they buy multiple products or upgrade to premium options - but even then, you can find an average without too much effort.

Taking the upgrade example: you might conclude that 80% of your customers stick to a basic product, so they're worth £1000 to you, as above. But 20% will upgrade after the first £50 sale, then spend an average of £100 per month and stay for 5 years.

So customers in that smaller segment are worth £6050 (100 x 5 x 12, + 50).

Now put those numbers together. 80% of customers are worth £1000, 20% are worth £6050, so a set of 100 customers brings you £201,000. That gives you an average lifetime value of £2010.

 Hopefully, this exercise will unearth a profitable customer and product combination. But the key word there is *profitable.*

Is there enough profit in your average customer to warrant spending money recruiting more of the same?

If not, this is a good time to review your pricing - or dig deeper and find a more profitable mix.

## 9. Flesh out your customer profile

So far, we've used broad definitions, like "Single Women", for your customer types. But now you've identified your best type, it's time to flesh out the definition - and possibly break the group down into smaller sub-groups.

As an example, let's stay with "Single Women". With further analysis, you might find that a high portion of the group will have other things in common. Maybe there's a sub-group of women who are aged 35-44, live in North London, own small dogs and love travelling? If so, that information will be enormously valuable when it comes to buying new data and writing your sales letter copy.

The easiest way to build this type of detail into your customer profile is to share your database with a data mining company. The Database Partnership, DBS Data, Experian and others have vast amounts of data that's been collected through research and delivery of services. So they can "retro-profile" your data and give you a wide range of insights.

For consumer mailings, match types include age, gender, lifestyle, income, property type, profession, interests and buying patterns like response to other direct marketing and mail order campaigns.

For business mailings, match types include industry sector, turnover, employee base, location and subscription to specific industry publications.

## 10. Find a list broker

By now, you've learned a lot about your best customer type (or types). You know what products they buy and how much they're worth to your business, and you've gained other insights to give you some background. That's a good point to start looking for a list broker.

If you've gone through the data profiling exercise in the last step, talk to the people who did the work for you - there's every chance they'll be able to supply reliable new data with similar match types.

If they can't help - or if you've skipped the exercise - you'll need to find a reputable broker who can take your insights and supply a responsive list.

**'Reputable' is the key word here, because the data industry is plagued by rogue suppliers. Making the wrong choice could lead to all kinds of problems. The most common being:**

- Outdated records. Mailing lists degrade at a rate of 10% every year, so if you buy a list that's 3-5 years old, the level of wastage could easily spell the difference between profit and loss.

- Unreliable data gathering. If records are compiled manually, through amateur sources like trawling the phone book or Google listings, you'll end up with a 'hit and miss' list with too many unsuitable records.

- MPS Violations. All mailing data should be cross-matched with MPS – the Mailing Preference Service that allows consumers to reject unsolicited mail at source. Anyone who's signed up to MPS will be quick to report abuses, which can lead to regulatory problems.

Thankfully, it's easy to spot low quality lists, because they're usually cheap. You'll be offered tens of thousands of records for a flat fee of just a few hundred pounds. It might seem like a bargain, but the low response and delivery rates will cost you dear.

The easiest way to avoid this pitfall is to check out the **UK Direct Marketing Association**. Brokers who belong to this body have signed up to a set of standards for data collection and maintenance - including a maximum tolerance of 5% non-delivery.

For more information, see the DMA's website: **www.dma.org.uk**.

## 11. Compile a suitable list

A good broker has access to millions of names and addresses - and each record is tagged with insights like consumer demographics and business SIC codes. Not only that, they have access to thousands of mailing lists - mostly drawn from other mailers and publishers who rent the data from their own campaigns.

Putting these two assets together, a broker can find people who have a known interest in your type of product...then overlay the data to highlight actual buyers...and overlay again to highlight people who match your target demographics. So when you mail out to the filtered list, you know the odds are stacked in your favour.

This sounds easy. However, there's a lot of room for error so it's vital that you agree a set of criteria first.

35

Let's create a scenario, for illustration. Say you're promoting a new natural supplement, to help people who suffer from back pain, with a price tag of £200 for the first course of treatment. So you tell your list broker to find a list of people with back pain. He obliges by pulling some data together from a few different mailing campaigns, and filters the list so it matches your customer profile. Finally, he confirms that everyone on the list has responded to a previous campaign and made at least one purchase relating to back pain.

At first glance, it's easy to think that list is good to go. But it's not - it could still contain all kinds of unsuitable records.

Firstly, we have to ask if the people on the list are a good match for the product. Yes, they've bought something to cure back pain, but what was it? A natural remedy? Non-prescription drugs? Magnetic therapy? Chiropractic or physio treatment? An acupuncture kit?

All these things are classed as treatments for back pain, but is that enough of a match? Someone who buys non-prescription drugs or chiropractic treatment is not an obvious prospect for a natural supplement. So for best results, you'd need to filter the list so you only reach people who have tried other natural remedies.

Secondly, there's the question of price. It stands to reason, if you're selling a remedy for £200, a list of people who bought a £10 product is little or no use. So now you'd filter again, so you only reach the people who bought a premium item.

Thirdly, and finally, there's the buying behaviour of the prospect. Ideally, you're looking for serial buyers - eternal optimists who keep trying new remedies - because they're the most likely people to give you a fair hearing. You won't persuade the person who bought a natural remedy once and decided it wasn't for him. And similarly, the person who's repeatedly bought the same product will be too set in his ways. So that's one more filter needed before you sign off the list.

As you can see, it's easy to miss a step in this process – then you could end up excluding good prospects or letting the wrong people in. So when you and your broker agree the criteria for your list, you need to account for the people you don't want as much as those you do.

## 12. Find the passion in the list

This is a step that most marketers - and even brokers - ignore, but one that can make a sizeable difference. It works especially well in consumer mailings for grudge purchases: something the prospect needs but won't get excited about, like insurance or a new boiler.

This is how it works. Let's say you've found 10,000 records that match your customer profile - so you know they're likely to need your product, and they'll have the means to buy it.

What you don't know is, *what else makes them tick?* What's the seemingly unrelated thing that's sure to grab their attention...and is it something you can use to good effect in your mailing?

Example: let's say you sell life insurance and you find that 500 people (5% of your list) are interested in golf. That's priceless information, because they don't want to read about life insurance - but they do want to read about golf. So if you can tie golf into your insurance mailer, you've got a shortcut to their attention.

Tying it in is easy. Offer a golf-based promotion like a prize draw for tickets to a major event. Or build the message around an image of someone on a golf course, with a caption like "You're fully covered - now relax and do your own thing".

Similarly, another 5% of your list could be avid travellers, or wine lovers, or classical music fans...and each passion can be tied into the mailer in the same way. Of course, a percentage of your list will need a vanilla version of the mailer, because you can't tie in their passion. But for the rest, you can segment the data and send a mailing that instantly pushes their buttons.

**Your whole campaign hinges on the quality of your mailing list. So while this first stage can be complex and demanding, it's worth persevering. Your effort will be rewarded.**

SECTION 2:

# Planning The Campaign

**By now you've chosen your list, and a product to promote. But there's still the matter of strategy - the why and how that drives your campaign.**

So in this section, we'll cover the main points to consider before you sit down and create your mailer.

## 13. Planning for long-term profits

Back in Step 9, we looked at a few examples of customer lifetime value. Dust off your figures now, because the conclusions you drew will help you plan your mailing.

Let's say you're selling a monthly package, with this lifetime value equation:

- Frequency: 12 sales per year

- Value: £100 per sale

- Direct cost of each sale £30

- Lifespan: 3 years

- Customer Lifetime Sales Value: £3,600

- Customer Lifetime Profitability: £2,520

The question now is, *how much are you willing to spend to bring in the £3600 customer?*

You'll have overheads like data, print, fulfilment and postage...and possibly some creative costs like hiring a copywriter or graphic designer. So before you do anything else, decide - what's an acceptable cost of sale?

There's no right or wrong answer here, but the smart response is to look beyond the first sale and focus on lifetime value. If the first sale makes a small loss or breaks even, that's an acceptable cost - because you know the typical customer will stay with you and spend more in the long term.

So let's say that you want to break even after the second month. In that case, your acceptable cost of sale is 2 months' worth of sales – that's £200 (less of course your costs of product £60).

Now multiply that across the campaign. Assume you're testing on a small scale first by mailing to 1000 people - and you're targeting a 2% response, which means 20 new customers. Therefore your budget is £140 x 20, which equals £2,800 (or £2.80 per letter mailed).

That gives you enough leeway to develop a strong mailer, using good copy and design, plus a quality paper stock.

If you stick to that budget...and you get the target response...you'll recoup your investment in Month 2.  And more importantly, you'll have 20 new customers who will each spend a further £2,380. A lifetime profit: £47,600.

That's the theory. But in practice, what happens if your response is lower than you hoped?

Don't panic. Let's say you get a 1% response (10 new customers). That's fine. Your response is halved, so your cost of sale doubles...meaning that you won't break even until Month 4. But that still gives you 10 customers, each spending a further £2,120. A lifetime profit: £21,200.

Conversely, your response could be higher - let's say it hits 4%. By doubling the response rate, your cost of sale is halved to £100. That gives you 40 customers, each spending a further £2,450. Total profit: £98,000.

Whatever the response, the key to success is focusing on the long term - knowing the lifetime value and having the confidence to set your targets around it. Your competitors won't dare to do this, because in their eyes a campaign that breaks even would be an abject failure! That's fine - it means you can out-spend them and make much more of an impact with your mailing.

Once you've tested and measured your mailer, you'll gain more confidence in both your response rates and customer lifetime value. Then you can afford to multiply your mailing cost many times over. With enough investment, you can create a 'shock and awe'

package that's guaranteed to grab the prospect's attention.

*More on this in Section 9.*

## 14. Don't set an annual budget

Once you know your campaign numbers, conventional thinking would be to build the campaign into an annual marketing plan - like sending the mailer out half a dozen times every year. But why would you do that when you know that your mailer is working for you *with predictable regularity*? Every time you mail out, you make more money. Building that into a finite plan is limiting the amount of money your business can generate.

Of course, some planning is necessary. You might need to plan your spending a few weeks ahead, or plan your resources to cope with demand. But that doesn't call for an annual plan or budget. It's far better to review your progress at the end of every month and decide what you'll be doing in the month ahead.

But even then though, don't be afraid to break away from the plan! If your resources allow it, why not give your sales a mid-month boost...or two?

## 15. Exploit your peak selling season

Back in Step 6, when we looked at the 80:20 Principle, you probably identified a 'silly season' when your sales go into overdrive. If so, you'll want to fully exploit the season - so be ready to saturate the market when it comes around.

It's worth pausing here to consider *why* your sales peak at this time of year. Most likely, there's a date or event in the calendar that acts as a trigger - examples being Christmas, Easter, New Year, sporting events, seasonal weather, school terms, Halloween, end of financial year and others. Identify the trigger and you can plan your mailings around it. You could also use it within your message - for example, use it as a reason for making a specific offer.

If there's no peak season in your business, there's another possibility - that your customers are acting in their own calendar cycle. For example, restaurant owners will see regular customers returning on birthdays and anniversaries. If this is a factor in your business, you'll need to gather relevant customer data and plan your mailings around each customer's personal dates.

## 16. Choose a response mechanism that suits the customer - not you

Take another look at your target customer type, and check how they came to you originally. Which sales or marketing channel brought them in - and what was the response mechanism at the time?

This is valuable intelligence, because your replica set of prospects will probably want to respond in the same way.

For example, say the first set answered a press or magazine advert. If they responded by phone - by calling an order or enquiry line - then it's safe to assume your replica set will respond to DM by phone. In which case, you should give them all the information they need within the mailer, ending with a phone number.

On the other hand, if the ad sent them to a website where they accessed more information and a sign-up page, your replica set may not be inclined to pick up the phone. In that case, you might fare better by mailing a postcard with a short teaser message and web link - so they complete the process online.

This type of integrated online/offline campaign can be very effective. You get the attention-grabbing value of a DM piece, coupled with the interactivity of a web page. You can flesh out the online part of the message using images and video, and offer a 1-click step to a purchase or enquiry.

## 17. Trial a Personal URL (pURL)

The Personalised URL is a highly effective, and much under-used, device. The principle is that you create a web page exclusively for the prospect - so their name features in the web address itself, in a salutation at the top of the page and anywhere else you want to include it, like the call to action.

You can also personalise other elements, depending on how much you know about the prospect.

Tests have repeatedly shown that pURLS increase readership, especially when the address is sent through the mail. A postcard with a short teaser message works especially well.

What's more, a pURL allows you to track the prospect's journey online - so if they click away from the personal page to visit a product page of your website, you know they're interested in that product. Then, if they don't buy, you can add them to a dedicated follow-up funnel where you focus more acutely on one solution.

Choose a personal URL that conveys action or a benefit, like JohnSmith.MakesMillions.com.

Capitalise each word, so it's easy to read – and keep the whole string short so it's easy to type.

You could also add a QR code, so readers can scan the letter with a mobile app and leap straight to a mobile web page.

## 18. Follow Up Relentlessly

Historically, we were told it takes between 7 - 12 points of contact before someone is willing to buy. But today, with the constant deluge of commercial messages, that's increased. The figure now is more like 20 - 30 times. So be persistent!

Of course, you can't continue mailing forever - there comes a time when you have to give up. But a typical business gives up far too soon, usually after 2 or 3 points of contact. That's like digging a 9 foot hole when the treasure is buried 10 feet down.

A long follow-up sequence should include at least 3 actual mailshots - maybe something like this:

1)  Short letter, to capture the most likely prospects

2)  Long letter, to capture the bulk of prospects

3)  Postcard, to capture the procrastinators

The mailers can then be mixed with other messages, like emails, faxes, voice broadcasts and old-fashioned telesales.

If you've got the reader's email address, try following up with Facebook Ads. You can upload a list of email addresses to Facebook's Ad Creator, and show your ads to anyone whose account is linked to a matching address. Then your ads can remind them of the major benefits, or stress that the deadline is looming...with an invitation to click through to your order page.

You can also reach people who visited your web page but failed to take action, by using the Remarketing option in Facebook or Google. Remarketing adds a cookie to the

SECTION 2: PLANNING THE CAMPAIGN

reader's web browser, so they'll see your ads when they visit Facebook or sites on Google's Content Network. It all helps to lift your response rates, without adding too much to your budget.

Once you've weighed up all these options, you should be able to settle on a strategy that underpins your campaign. The next step is to create an offer that supports the strategy...

47

SECTION 3:

# Creating Your Offer

**Your mailer is an interruption. The prospect has begun their day with other things on their mind, and suddenly, in the middle of it all, your message arrives. You're trying to divert their attention away from all those urgent matters, and get them to focus on you instead. That's no easy task.**

Even if you get their attention, getting them to respond - and do it now - is a whole different challenge. Your only hope of success is to offer an incentive so they feel compelled to respond straight away, for fear of missing out.

So, in this section we'll look at ways to create an irresistible offer...

## 19. Lead generation or instant sale: decide now

Some of the most successful mailers make no attempt at selling. Instead, they offer something free, such as a book, report or video: something informative, that moves the customer one step closer to the sale and paves the way for a series of follow-up messages.

For example, take a bridal shop that's mailing to a list of women who are recently engaged. They could take the standard approach and mail a letter with a wedding dress catalogue, plus a special offer that's redeemable in-store. Or they could tell the reader about a brand new wedding guide, such as **7 Tips on Planning and Staging the Perfect Wedding**. All the reader has to do to request a copy is call a number or visit a web page. Then as a bonus, they'll be offered a private fitting session where they can try on dresses and find the perfect style – with no obligation.

With the first option, the message is clearly "Hurry, we want your business!" While in the second, the message is "We'd welcome the chance to show how we can help you". As a result, the customer will feel valued and respected...they'll come to trust the bridal store and value the owner's expertise...and the owner will have many chances to win the customer's business, by following up in a series of helpful letters and emails.

Sometimes, this is a much better method than selling straight off the page – especially if you're approaching a new prospect who's had no contact with you in the past.

 Is this the right approach for your customer type? If you're replicating the conditions of previous sales, lead generation could cause a shift in the pattern. If in doubt, test it against a regular sales letter – something we'll touch on later.

## 20. Choose your giveaway

If you're opting for lead generation, the first thing you need is a free gift for the prospect. Consider this:

1.  Your gift will be more appealing if it's a physical product like a book or DVD, rather than a virtual product like an eBook or YouTube clip. A physical product will also be retained, giving you long-term space on the reader's desk or coffee table.

2.  Don't send the free gift straight away – let the reader request it, so you're only spending extra on the people who show an interest.

3.  You might feel that you need to make a bigger offer, like a free sample product or free use of a service. This can work, but beware of giving too much away: there's a fine line between an irresistible offer and devaluing a product.

## 21. Identify your best responders

If you're torn between lead generation and immediate sale, there's an interim option that can give you the best of both worlds: offer something free, as above, then offer a premium version of your freebie for a token fee.

This is how it works. Your mailer sends the reader to a web page, where they can take advantage of the offer. No mention of the premium option yet, because your only goal right now is to get them to sign up for the free option.

Once they've completed their request, take them to a thank-you page where you offer the premium option. With some well-written sales copy – and perhaps a video - to push the added benefits, you'll find that a percentage of responders will happily take this option. That's good for you in two ways:

Firstly, the money from the sale will help to cover the cost of the mailing - including the cost of the original giveaway. Depending on the numbers, it could cover the entire cost or even deliver a small profit. At the very least, it will speed your ROI - the return on the investment you make in your marketing.

Secondly, it gives you a two-tier list. In tier one, you'll have 'warm' prospects who just took the free option. And in tier two, you'll have 'hot' prospects - people who tell you they have a pressing need for your type of solution, who are ready to trust you already. When it comes to follow-up, you can push this group for bigger, faster sales.

## 22. Use purchase history to frame your offer

Lead generation is not your only option. There's nothing wrong with going straight for the sale – especially if you're targeting existing customers.

If that's your plan, be sure to use your customer's purchase data. You'll know what they've bought in the past, so you can predict the things they'll want to buy in the future. Think of

Amazon, and the way they recommend books and other items, just by using the principle "If you liked that, you'll like this".

If you went through the profiling exercises in Section 1, it should be easy for you to identify the best upsell products for your customer type. That could mean accessories, new parts, consumables, enhancements, replacements or upgrades.

There are agencies who can help you to make sense of purchase history and segment your customers into groups that qualify for specific offers. You don't have to go it alone.

## 23. Added value beats a discount

There are 2 ways to make a sales offer: discount the price or add some extra value to the standard price. The latter is always better. To explain why, let's look at a product that sells for £100.

*The Discount Option*
You halve the price, selling 20 units for £50 each. Net value: £1000. Plus, you've got 20 new customers who you can sell to again.

*The Added Value Option*
You stick to the price and add some extra goodies. So you sell 10 units for £100 each. Net value £1000, minus the cost of the extras. Plus, you've got 10 new customers who you can sell to again.

On the surface, the discount option looks better.

It gives you twice as many new customers, and you don't have the extra cost of providing a bonus.

But dig a little deeper and you'll see that's a false economy...

*First, the bonus:*
- It could be something you've already got lying around, that's taking up space in your warehouse - so you can supply it with no extra cost bar postage and packaging.

- It could be a second widget (like 2 for 1 or 3 for 2) that you can afford to offer without destroying your margins*.

- Or it could be some kind of information that you deliver electronically. Then there's no cost at all – and if it shows the customer why they need some other product you sell, the bonus generate its own revenue.

In other words...providing a bonus is easy - and it could even be an asset.

*Second, the customer issue: 10 customers Vs 20:*
- The 10 customers who pay £100 will be looking for value rather than savings. That's the mindset of a good customer.

---

*The offer of a 2nd item at a reduced price commonly increases the average value of your orders by 20%. Typically, it will increase your profit margin by even more as you have no additional marketing costs – your only overheads are supply and delivery.

- In contrast, the 20 customers who pay £50 are likely to be opportunists, who buy on price. They won't appreciate value, and they won't show you loyalty...they'll just desert you as soon as someone else offers a better deal.

Remember, the real profit is in the long term – not the first sale. And 10 high spending customers looking for value and quality should be worth more to you than 20 bargain-hunters.

## 24. Add an early bird bonus

Make your offer, then improve it for people who respond by a certain date. As above, it doesn't have to be a discount - just something that's too good to resist.

When you make this type of offer, it's best to see it as the main deadline. So your follow-up messages should intensify as the early bird date approaches, then slow to a trickle afterwards.

A physical mailing after the early bird date is unlikely to be cost effective - so at that stage, it's better to rely on email and other low-cost channels.

## 25. Offer a premium standard

Most of your customers will just want the basic offer. But there's always a percentage who want something more, and would gladly pay the extra. Don't miss this opportunity.

Your premium service could include enhancements to a product, or other things designed to make the customer's life easier. Think around your product, including the things that the customer needs before and after they use it. Where can you add value?

This doesn't have to mean adding a new string to your bow. You can easily do it in partnership with another business. For example, if you're a travel operator, your premium could be a chauffeur service that takes customers to and from the airport. All you have to do is find a local supplier and agree a fee for passing them business. It costs you nothing to offer or deliver the service, so your fee is 100% profit.

**Keep choices to a minimum**

It's tempting to throw in all kinds of offers, to make sure there's something for everyone. But if you give too much choice, readers will get confused and put your letter to one side while they weigh up their options.

Your best bet is a single offer, with a premium option. Anything more than this and your responses will start to dip.

If you feel the need to make multiple offers, it might be a sign that you need to segment your list and send separate mailers to different customer types.

# 26. Create a reason for the offer

By and large, a customer who's genuinely interested will want to believe that your offer is the real deal. But they'll have a voice in their head telling them there must be a catch. So they'll want your help to silence the nagging doubt.

You can oblige by telling them why you're making the offer.

Some reasons are overused. Consumers have heard enough about stock clearances, fire or flood damage and making way for new lines! So don't invent a reason - be honest. Think why you're making the offer, and share it with the reader – perhaps in the form of a story, to get them involved. *(More on stories in section 6).*

## 27.    An offer without a deadline isn't an offer at all

An offer cuts both ways: you're making a concession, but the reader will only get it if they act right away. So make sure you add some form of urgency to the offer, like a deadline or limited number before stock runs out or prices rise.

Again, make sure it's genuine. Readers can always sniff out BS! And stick to your word - if you offer something past a deadline, no-one will believe you next time around.

 Lengthy deadlines kill response. For your first letter, set your deadline 5 – 14 days from the date of mailing. Then follow up a few days later, and send a final reminder 1-2 days before the deadline.

If you're using scarcity, the same principle holds true: don't offer too many units at the offer price. Test different numbers to find the best option.

## 28. Don't fear the guarantee

Sometimes the only thing holding a customer back is fear of the unknown - a fear that a purchase will backfire somehow. So take the risk away by offering a full and unconditional guarantee.

This is another of those seemingly brave moves that your competitors would never consider - so do this and you'll stand out in your market as the safest option.

There's no need to shy away from this, because the simple truth is, any business that gives genuine value will profit from making a bold guarantee. Of course, occasional customers will demand their money back, so you'll lose out here and there. But overall, the uplift you'll get from making the guarantee will more than compensate for the small number of refunds.

Decided on your offer? Now let's get on with the task of planning your message...

# SECTION 4:

# Planning The Message

So far, so good. You've narrowed down your audience and created an offer – so it's almost time to sit down and write your letter. But before you do, it's worth taking a few moments to plan out the message: what are you going to say, and how?

## 29. Use the AIDA structure

There are hundreds of different ways to structure a sales letter – but by far the most reliable is AIDA: Attention, Interest, Desire, Action.

**Attention:** your headline makes a promise, telling the reader that they'll benefit from reading on. So it gets them to stop what they were doing, and focus on your message.

**Interest:** you keep the reader hooked by expanding on the promise. You might jump straight in, by describing your solution straight away...or you might go back a few steps, by first describing the reader's problem and how it affects their life. A story that ties into your product works especially well here.

**Desire:** you describe the benefits of your solution, and how it will make life better – using emotive language and bullet points that hammer home the advantages. Build the reader's desire by giving them reasons to believe you, in the form of testimonials or other proof.

**Action:** make your offer...and make it irresistible. Then tell the reader how to claim it – reminding them of the pleasure ahead, and the pain they'll suffer if they ignore your offer.

**This is a broad structure that you can use now to plan out your message. Then in the sections that follow, we'll look at some individual techniques for grabbing attention with headlines, increasing desire and more.**

# 30. Test a different structure

AIDA works in just about any situation – selling to customers or prospects, whether they're warm or cold, and for any type of product or service.

It should work for you. But if it doesn't, try one of these alternatives:

**Problem-Agitate-Resolve**
This is a very simple and powerful 3-part formula:

**Problem:** focus on the customer's pain, as a way of grabbing their attention.

**Agitate:** twist the knife, showing the impact of living with the problem – now and in the long term.

**Resolve:** offer to take the pain away, by introducing your solution.

This formula works for any type of product, but it's especially useful for grudge purchases: insurance, car servicing, home maintenance, warrantees and other things that you only buy because you have to.

**5 x P**

A slightly longer formula, that's rarely used – but highly effective:

**Picture:** get the reader to imagine the end result, of a dream life with your solution in place.

**Promise:** connect the dream to reality – tell them that it could happen, despite their natural misgivings.

**Product:** introduce your solution: what sets it apart, and why it can make good on your promise.

**Proof:** silence nagging doubts with testimonials and credentials.

**Purchase:** make your offer and tell the reader what to do next.

This formula works especially well for products that help customers follow their dreams   - like luxury items or breakthrough solutions to age-old problems.

# 31. Short or long copy? You decide

How long should your sales letter be? This debate has been raging among copywriters and marketers for generations, and chances are it won't end any time soon. The easy answer is, long copy normally out-performs short copy - but that doesn't tell the whole story. Here are some points to consider:

(1) You won't bore the reader with long copy - you'll bore them with dull copy. An exciting 20-pager will command more attention than a dull single page!

(2) There's no need to overwrite something, just so the message is "long!" Long copy works when you say everything you need to say...but when you've said it all, it's time to stop.

(3) Length of copy depends on what you're asking the reader to do. Clearly, they'll need a ton of information before they'll buy a £10k widget, but not so much before they'll spend £10. Similarly, if you're not asking for money, copy can be shorter again - so a lead generation piece, where you pitch for an email address, can often benefit from the rule that "less is more".

(4) If your mailer is a teaser piece that sends people online, the length of your letter is only one part of the puzzle – you should also test the length of your landing page copy.

(5) Some recent tests have shown that younger people respond well to short copy online – especially when they're browsing via a mobile. However, this is a radical shift from traditional thinking, so you should test it in your own business before leaping to conclusions.

 The key to long copy is creating what's known as a Dual Reader Path – a layout that lets readers find their own way through the message. They can read it from start to finish, or just race through the important points by picking out headlines, sub-headings, images, bullet points and highlighted text. We'll be looking at each of these techniques in more detail.

## 32. Personalise it!

One of the great things about digital printing is that you can create personalised letters for the cost of mailing in bulk. Your printer is already personalising the reader's name and address, so why not add some extra fields and make the letter more personal?

At a basic level, you might split your database by age, demographic or gender - then vary the colours or images to reflect a certain lifestyle.

But that's only the start. The more you know about the reader, the more you can personalise. For example:

• Pre-populate your letter or order form with the customer's last order item and value.

• Tailor an upsell offer or bonus that fits with the customer's buying history.

• Use their job title or hobby: reference it and talk about specific challenges, as a lead-in to your offer.

- Find out what they're interested in, by checking contact records, tagging email click-throughs, or buying in targeted data...then drop in relevant copy, like a guarantee, offer or testimonial that tackles their needs or objections.

By adding this kind of data, you stand to gain on 2 levels: first, you have a better chance of pushing the customer's buttons, because you're hitting their visual cues and addressing relevant issues. And secondly, you're showing the customer that you recognise them as an individual - so they'll respect you more than the person who sends them something bland and generic.

You can use personalisation as a tracking tool. Generate personal voucher codes or personal URLs, and you can create instant reports to show where your sales have come from.

Better yet, if you cross-reference your tracking with other forms of personalisation, you can identify patterns across your database:

- How do sales vary by age, gender and other demographics?
- Which products or packages get repeat sales or upgrades?
- Which parts of the country spend the most money?

Whatever you want to find out about your customers, personalisation can help.

Run an electronic test with your data to make sure all your variable fields populate correctly. You needn't check your whole database – the first 10 to 20 letters should be enough. Just review each customised page and verify that all salutations are correct. If you see delimiters like 'FName' or 'SName', go back to your database and mail merge system to cancel out the errors.

# 33. Get endorsed by a celebrity

Celebrities are pre-approved by the general public - so if one endorses your business, they'll add massive credibility.

The key, of course, is finding a celebrity who fits the bill. You need someone who is:

- Liked, admired and trusted by your target audience (perhaps a local hero)

- Free and willing to take part in some form of promotion

- Not working with a rival brand, or tied up with other endorsements

- A natural fit for your product - because they share your values, or your business has helped them in some way

Once you've identified a good candidate, getting them to say yes might be easier than you think. Even well-known faces can find themselves in and out of work, and would happily boost their income by adding their name to a product they can believe in.

What's more, hiring them needn't cost too much. You may just end up paying for a few days of their time, to cover photo shoots, or a video shoot for a web page - plus a retainer or percentage share of incremental sales.

In some cases, they may work for nothing! For example, if you're a charity, they'll enjoy the PR of supporting a good cause. And in other cases, they might accept a contra deal. If you're a builder, you could offer to build their extension in exchange for an endorsement. It happens.

 Celebrity endorsement is most effective in the consumer market. If you sell to businesses, celebrities carry less weight. But you can get the same effect by hiring well-known business or public figures, or serious broadcasters. (Even former MPs and newsreaders have to eat!)

## 34. Choose your internal authors carefully

If you're using a celebrity, it stands to reason they should act as the author of any sales or lead generation letter. But if you're just using an internal author - the business owner or a member of staff - you'll need to choose carefully.

If you're targeting new prospects, your Managing Director is the best choice by far. The worst choice - at least in the UK - is your Sales Director. For some reason, the British have an in-built resistance to sales, so we're more likely to place our trust in a more 'noble' figure like the MD!

Once you get to customer communications, the game changes a little. The MD is still useful for major announcements, but for general communication your best author is your Head of Customer Services. By leading with them, you're telling the customer that service is the heart of your business - so much so that they'll be effective for upsell messages too.

If you're selling a sensitive item – like a weight loss or medical product – readers may prefer to deal with someone of their own gender. So if you're producing different versions for male and female readers, try varying the signatory and see how it affects your response.

## 35. The more response methods, the better

In section 3, when we looked at offers, we noted that you shouldn't overwhelm customers with too much choice: just make a standard offer, with perhaps a premium option.

However, when it comes response methods, the opposite is true: more choice is better than less, because we all feel comfortable responding in different ways.

As a minimum, offer a telephone number plus an order form with reply envelope. Then add other options to suit your market. Readers who grew up without the internet still respond well to cut-out coupons, while readers of the web generation often prefer to sign up online.

In fact, this is a perfect place to use a pURL – a Personal URL – as we've already covered. If the reader sees that the web page has been created just for them, they're much more likely to visit.

You'll want to know where your sales come from, so make sure every response method is trackable. If you use a coupon, add an offer code. If you give out a telephone number, make it unique. We'll look at measurement in more detail in Section 12.

## 36. Responding should be free

If you make the customer pay to contact you, your response rate is bound to suffer. So your phone number should be free - or at least local rate - and your reply envelope should be pre-paid. Don't lose a valuable prospect for the sake of a few pennies.

Of course, for registered charities, free postage can be a stretch too far. But you still have options:

- Give people the choice: let them use a FREEPOST envelope, or help your cause further by adding a stamp.

OR:

- Apply for a special mail allowance: a discount rate that's reserved for the not-for-profit sector. Your mailing house should discuss this with you at the start of your project.

People also hate paying for delivery. Even a small charge for postage and packaging can make them re-think the value of the product. So consider absorbing the delivery cost, or building it into the sales price.

You can always test this, to see how people respond to different options

**Once you've made these last few decisions, you're ready to start writing your letter...**

## SECTION 5:

# Grabbing Attention with Headlines

**If you want readers to respond, you need to get their attention first!**

**So to begin, you need a powerful headline that makes them sit up and take notice.**

A headline works as a kind of information filter. We're all busy, and we're all bombarded with sales messages all day long, so we can't possibly take in everything we see. Hence, we use headlines to decide what to read and what to ignore.

That makes your headline the single most important part of your mailer. So we'll spend this section looking at proven ways to get it right...

### 37. Check your customer insights

By now, you should know an enormous amount about your target customer. You'll know what matters to them, what keeps them awake at night, what they fantasise and worry about...and how your product can change their work or home life for the better.

These insights are your best weapons when it comes to writing your headline, because they help you to get inside the customer's head. If you know what they long for, a headline can promise to make it happen. If you know what they fear, promise to help them avoid it. If you know why they're sceptical, break down their resistance.

In other words, use your knowledge to get their attention and give them a reason to read on.

If you get to this stage and feel you still don't know them well enough, now is the time to gather more insights. Try talking to customers, or polling them with tools like Survey Monkey, or just reviewing the comments they leave on forums and social media pages.

Or if you know someone who 'fits the mould' of your target customer, talk to them. What matters to them? What do you have to say to make them sit up and listen?

The better you know your customer, the better your chance of touching a raw nerve. So don't skip this process. Find out everything you can, from their choice of newspaper to the kind of words they use in everyday conversation.

## 38. Know your USP

Every company has (or should have!) a unique selling proposition: that thing that sets you apart from the competition. It should be something meaningful, relevant and specific. But most companies opt for something generic -

usually either "We're the cheapest" or "We're the best". And that's not wise.

"We're the cheapest" is a dangerous boast. Firstly, because you're inviting people who buy on price - and they tend to be difficult, disloyal customers who expect the earth. And secondly, because you're inviting others to undercut you - and you'll end up racing each other to the bankruptcy courts! Pricing is a vast topic in its own right, and we can't cover it here in detail. But as we've said already, the sensible thing is to focus on value - not nickels and dimes.

As for "We're the best", well that's a claim every business makes - to the point that it just washes over the reader. They won't believe it unless you can prove it through testimonials and case studies - showing exactly *why* you're better than all the others out there.

If you're stuck, here are 3 easy ways to develop a USP:

(1) Ask your best customers: why did they buy from you first time, and why do they keep coming back?

> Example: maybe they liked your personal touch, or the way you go the extra mile. Whatever your strength is, build on it...take it as far as you can, so your competitors become the poor man's alternative.

(2) Become the antidote: think of all the things that people hate or distrust in your industry, and become the supplier who doesn't do those things.

> Example: if you're a management consultant, your market is known for using business speak and getting lost in management theory. So your USP could be practical solutions, delivered in plain English.

(3) Compare apples with oranges: create a product that's different from the rest. Try bundling things together, piling on the value, or adding a strong guarantee - then customers will struggle to compare you side by side with others.

> Example: if you run a laundry service, offer free pick-up and delivery. Or guarantee that you'll replace or repair damaged items. Or offer a bundled tailoring service, for repairs and alterations.

Any one of these methods – or a combination – can set your business apart.

Once you know your USP and your customer, you're ready to start writing headlines.

## 2 world class USPs:

**FedEx:** 'When it absolutely, positively has to be there overnight'

**Domino's:** 'Pizza Delivered in 30 Minutes or it's Free'

## 39. Sell the message – not the product

Your headline can't make the sale. No-one is going to read a sentence or two and decide to buy right away...so don't even try to close the deal here.

The only thing you can sell in a headline is the message itself. Give the reader a reason to read on, then develop your pitch further down.

*That's the principle. So, how do you do it...?*

## 40. Offer a solid benefit

Perhaps the easiest way to write a headline is to answer the customer's question *What's In It For Me?*

Unfortunately, many people (even some copywriters) get side-tracked here and start describing features instead of actual benefits. So before we go any further, let's set a definition:

*A feature is the thing that your product does.*

*A benefit is how that feature changes things for the better.*

To put this another way, a feature is purely functional, while a benefit connects with your customer on an emotional level, by solving a problem or enhancing their life in some way.

Take an extendable table: the fact that a section of the table extends and folds away is a feature – it's purely functional. The benefit is that you can adapt it for different occasions – so

73

share an intimate dinner one night and a lavish dinner party the next. That gives you an emotional angle to lead with in your headline.

**Here are some famous headlines that lead with benefit statements:**

- Drop a Dress Size in 2 Weeks

- Discover The Fortune That Lies Hidden in Your Salary

- Erase 10 Years in 10 Minutes

- You Can Laugh at Money Worries – If You Follow This Simple Plan

- Today…Add $10,000 to Your Estate – For the Price of a New Hat

- New Shampoo Leaves Your Hair Smoother – Easier to Manage

- Lose weight and shape up – just by changing to these shoes!

- Never shave, wax or bleach again…

- "I Lost My Bulges…And Saved Money, Too"

- Free Book – Tells You 12 Secrets of Better Lawn Care

- "You Get the Most Sparkling Clean, Fresh and Fluffy Carpet Ever Seen – or It's Free!!!"

## 41. Share some news

If you can surprise or shock the reader, you've got their attention. So a "Did you know...?" type headline can work wonders. Just think about what they're likely to know, then consider what they *should* know...and somewhere between the two, you've got some vital information to share.

Very often, that news will come through regulations or technology. Regulation means a new hoop to jump through, or some new entitlement they should be aware of. New technology, like a product revamp, means there's something readers can do today that they couldn't do before.

But just as often, the news is some kind of secret or a little-known fact. It could have been around for centuries...all that matters is that it comes as news to the reader, and that it could change their life for better or worse. Hence they need your help.

Just one caveat: if you're announcing news in your headline, deliver it tactfully. Readers don't warm to smugness or scare tactics – as used in this headline by a desperate Will Writer:

**GET THIS - New Government Tax Plans Will Eat Up Your Estate *And Spit It Out*
When You Die, <u>Unless You Change Your Will TODAY</u>. Do You Want Your Kids Begging on the Streets? Eating out of Dustbins? No – THEN CALL ME NOW!!**

The writer comes across as the happy bearer of bad news, who's exploiting a tax change in order to tout for business. There's nothing wrong with the strategy of sharing important news, but his phrasing should be more respectful – as in:

## How Is Your Will Affected by the Government's Latest Tax Plans?

*A Free 1-Hour Review Could Save*
*Your Family Tens of Thousands*

Of course, tone of voice depends on who you're writing to...it's possible that a certain audience might be okay with the first version! But as a rule, the second version will be much better received.

**Here are some successful headlines that lead with a piece of news:**

- Why Some Foods "Explode" in Your Stomach

- Baby Boomers Now Fear Memory Loss More Than Cancer

- Announcing...The New Edition of the Encyclopaedia That Makes It Fun to Learn Things

- Amazing Fat Fighting Smoothie Triggers Rapid Weight Loss...Even If You Cheat!

- Here's a Quick Way to Break Up a Cold

- Florida Eye Doctor Helps Legally Blind To See Again

- What Everybody Ought to Know...About This Stock and Bond Business

- The Amazing Money-Making Secret Of A Desperate Nerd From Ohio!

- Scientists Predict End of Obesity by 2018

## 42. Pique the reader's curiosity

Remember, you're not making the sale here - you just want the reader to carry on reading. And one way to do that is to tease, with just enough information to lure them in.

Newspaper headline writers are masters of this art. They know that if they say too little or too much, they'll lose the reader, so they have to find that perfect balance.

For example, let's say an actor from *Eastenders* gets arrested for drunk driving and claims someone else was at the wheel. A novice headline writer would aim to tell the whole story – as in:

### Eastenders' Joe Bloggs Arrested for Drunk Driving
### *Soap Star Protests His Innocence*

Or maybe they'll aim to tease, but offer too little – as in:

### Actor Arrested

But a more seasoned writer would find the balance – as in:

## Arrested Soap Star Insists 'I Wasn't Behind The Wheel'

The first example gives too much away, so why should the reader carry on? The second example doesn't offer enough to make the reader care. But the third example is about right – it hints at the details, leaving the reader to wonder which soap, which actor and what happened. Result: they'll want to read on...

Of course, you're not trying to write a newspaper headline. But you can use the exact same principle to tap into your reader's natural sense of curiosity. For example, you could:

...Hint at what they'll achieve, but stop short of telling them how.

...Suggest that they might qualify for an amazing - but limited - offer.

...Promise to share a secret that will change their life.

...Or start telling a story that they'll identify with.

**Here are some well-known headlines that lead with curiosity:**

- "I panicked...My hair was thinning!"

- How I Made a Fortune with a "Fool Idea"

- "Last Friday...Was I Scared! - My Boss Almost Fired Me!"

- A Wonderful Two Years' Trip at Full Pay – But Only Men with Imagination Can Take It

- Only One Cooker Comes With Emotional Baggage

- You're Going to Love This Amazing Deal...Unless You're a Traffic Warden!

- There is now a treatment that can significantly relieve the torment of <u>knee pain</u>. Without drugs. Without surgery. Would you like to know more?

## 43. Speak to the reader's self-esteem

We're a vain and insecure species! So many of the most successful headlines in history have delivered a killer blow by targeting the reader's sense of self-worth: their hidden ambitions, fears and insecurities that they'd never discuss with another person...but they'd gladly read about (when nobody's looking!).

**Here are some classic headlines that play on self-esteem:**

- How to Win Friends and Influence People

- They Laughed When I Sat Down at the Piano – But When I Started to Play!

- Do You Make These Mistakes in Job Interviews?

- Are You Ever Tongue-Tied at a Party?

- Have You a "Worry" Stock?

- Suppose This Happened on Your Wedding Day!

- Do You Do Any of These Ten Embarrassing Things?

- Have You Ever Had a "Senior Moment"?

- Imagine Me...Holding an Audience Spellbound for 30 Minutes

## 44. Call out to the reader

Often, you can strengthen your headline by adding a short line at the top, in a smaller front. This is sometimes referred to as a call-out statement, because it tells the reader at a glance that you're talking to them.

There are 3 main ways to write a call-out statement:

**...Identify the reader as part of a group – as in:**

- Important News for Small Business Owners

- Cat Lovers - Please Read Immediately

- "Opera Buffs Will Love This"

**...Address the reader's problem or aspiration – as in:**

- Fuel bills too high?

- Looking to retire within 10 years?

- Need Some Cash Fast? Try This...

- Depressed About BACK PAIN?

**...Or combine the first 2 methods, in a 'Group With Problem' statement – as in:**

- Accountants - do you need more clients?

- Exclusive opportunity for cyclists living with back pain

- To Men Who Want to Quit Work Someday

# 45. Add a 'Kicker'

A kicker is a statement that sits close to the headline, giving the reader an extra reason or two to read on. It could be a traditional sub-heading, or a bullet list, or it could be built into the design - maybe set in a circle or star.

For instance, let's take one of our headlines from earlier:

**Drop a Dress Size in 2 Weeks**

You could write a kicker for this headline in any number of ways. For example, you could:

**...Clarify the headline, with some basic 'what?' or 'who?' info – as in:**

- The New Fitness DVD That's Giving Slimmers New Hope

**...Expand on the headline, by describing what lies ahead – as in:**

- See amazing results in just 10 minutes a day

**...Give the product an air of respect, to help the reader believe – as in:**

- A Secret Regime - Direct from Hollywood's A-List Personal Trainer

**...Make it seem easy, by taking away the usual obstacles – as in:**

- No strenuous workouts. No crash diets. The common sense approach.

**...Or simply trail a major feature and benefit – as in:**

- Includes a Zero Diet Guide To Staying in Shape for the Long Haul

No matter how good your headline is, you'll probably improve it with a strong kicker. Give it a try...

# 46. Test Power Words

Some words are more powerful than others. 'Free' is stronger than 'Complimentary'. 'Discover' is better than 'Learn'. 'Now' is better than 'Presently'. Instinctively, that's something we all know - but it's worth remembering when you write copy, and especially the headline.

The most powerful words relate to the things we want most in this world, like love, money, respect, simplicity and privilege.

The following list of power words is certainly not definitive - but add one or two to your headline and it can make a real difference:

| | | |
|---|---|---|
| Adore | How To | Rapid |
| Amazing | Imagine | Results |
| Announcing | Immediate | Reveal |
| Astonishing | Important | Sad |
| At Last | Improve | Sale |
| Because | Insider | Save |
| Breakthrough | Instant | Secret |
| Cash | Introducing | Sensation |
| Caution | Killer | Simple |
| Confessions | Latest | Solve |
| Crazy | Limited | Strong |
| Desire | Look | Success |
| Discover | Lose | Surprising |
| Drop | Love | Tested |
| Easy | Magic | This |
| Extraordinary | Money | Today |
| Fast | New | Tonight |
| Fears | No Risk | Tragic |
| Final | Now | Unconditional |
| Finally | Offer | Unlimited |
| Feel | Phenomenal | Warning |
| Free | Powerful | Why |
| Guarantee | Proof | Winning |
| Hate | Proven | Yes |
| Healthy | Quick | You |

Most of the words on this list need no explanation. But there's one that might raise an eyebrow or two - that's the word 'Because'.

**'Because' is arguably the most powerful word in the English language, because....(hold that thought)**

Did you notice how your interest just peaked at the end of that last sentence? The word 'because' told you that some all-important information was coming, so chances are that (ever so subtly) your attention level rose.

This comes back to the point about giving your reason for making an offer...the more we understand the seller's motivation, the sooner we believe.

# 47. Use punctuation carefully

Punctuation marks can influence the reader's decision to quit or read on. They're only a small influence – they won't make or break your headline - but still, they can move your response rates up or down a notch.

This is how:

- **Full stops** tell readers to stop reading – so like a news editor, never add one at the end of a headline.

- **Commas** should be used sparingly, because they slow down the read, taking the edge off the headline.

- **Semi-colons** will only confuse; most people don't know what they are!

- **Brackets** delay the reader (see how this bracket is doing it right now) because they throw a second idea into the sentence. Better to keep it simple.

- **Exclamation marks** are the written equivalent of waving a finger in someone's face!! Yes, they can work now and again, to emphasise a point or inject some personality - but overdo it and readers will feel you're invading their personal space!!!

Exclamation marks are like BLOCK CAPITALS - some audiences accept them, and some find them invasive. As a rule, tabloid readers and younger readers are more at home with this type of aggressive writing.

BUT, whoever you're writing to, there's always a limit – because if you emphasise everything, you're emphasising nothing!!!

So, if possible, limit punctuation in your headline. If you're writing a longer sentence, try bridging it with a hyphen ( - ) or ellipsis ( ... ), as they help to link ideas and encourage the reader to carry on.

## 48. Write a selection, and choose the best

Once you've written a headline you can use, it's tempting to move on. But you should stay with it, until you have at least half a dozen solid options.

Don't worry if it takes you a while. Toy with ideas. Play with benefits, news, self-esteem and curiosity. Then set the work aside for a day, before you choose the best one.

Your efforts won't be wasted, because you can use your other headlines in split tests *(see section 10)*.

**Top copywriters spend half their writing time on headlines. Because they know, if they don't grab the reader's attention, there's zero chance of a response. So stay with this step until you've got a headline you can work with...then move on and start writing the letter.**

SECTION 6:

# Winning Them Over

**So you've got the reader's attention. They've made it past the headline, and now they're glancing at the rest of the page. So far, so good. Now your job is to set out your proposition and keep them on the hook...**

*Before we get into the structure of the letter, let's cover some general rules:*

## 49. Mind your salutation

The reader wants to feel that you're talking directly to them - so if your letter feels like a circular, they'll switch off straight away. For that reason, it's best to avoid generic salutations like "Dear Sir/Madam", "Dear Reader", "Dear Householder" or "Dear Friend".

If you can, use the reader's name, or identify them as part of a group - as in "Dear Stamp Collector" or "Dear Animal Lover".

If all else fails, try a simple "Hello" or "Hi There" to start the conversation on a friendly, informal footing.

## 50. Formality kills response

This is one of those hard and fast rules that simply can't be broken. The most successful sales letters in history have used a simple, natural tone that feels more like a conversation than a piece of writing. If you ignore this and write in a stiff and formal style, you'll be wasting a lot of money on a mailing that's doomed to failure. Sorry if that sounds harsh, but it's the way of things.

Just to be clear, it doesn't matter if you're selling B2b or B2c. And it doesn't matter if you're selling high end or bargain basement. People buy from people, so we all respond to a friendly, chatty style.

The rule is simple: write like you talk. Nothing else will work.

**There's more than one "conversational tone".**

We all have different ways of talking to different people. You have one way of talking to your best friends, another for older relatives, another for work colleagues, and another for superiors or clients.

It's all conversation, but your tone varies slightly from one audience to another.

Use that skill when you write your copy, to strike the right tone for your readers.

As a rule, you should always aim for informal or semi-formal – but exactly where you belong on the scale is a judgement call.

## 51. It's You, Not Me!

The reader isn't interested in you or your business - they only want to know what's in it for them. If you follow the points in this section, you'll automatically build some empathy and find that your focus shifts towards them - but still, it's worth policing your copy, just to be sure.

Some copywriters count the number of times they say "Me", "I", "We", "Us" and "Our" - then compare it with the number of times they say "You", "Your" and "Yours". The first list should be smaller, by a ratio of 1:3 or better. If it's not, then take another look and see how you can make it more about the reader, less about you.

**In practice, shifting from 'Me' to 'You' means:**

We can make a difference
*becomes:*
You'll see the difference

We'll take all your worries away
*becomes:*
You've got nothing to worry about

I know this is something you'll love
*becomes:*
You'll love this

**This is a very simple, but effective, technique. And if you couple it with the personalisation options we looked at in**

**Section 4, your letter will start to feel less like mass communication, more like a 1-2-1 message.**

## 52. Be careful with jargon

If you're writing to a specialist audience, you'll probably want to add some jargon or industry buzz words to show you're part of the crowd. That's fine - but keep in mind, there's a vital difference between jargon and formality. Ultimately, your copy should still be light and conversational.

If your readers are new to your subject, leave jargon well alone. It will cause confusion, and tell readers that you don't know or care about them.

If your readers are split between 'insiders' and 'outsiders', you need 2 versions of your letter – so segment your list and speak to each audience in their own language.

## 53. Use short sentences

Whoever you're writing to, it's always best to keep your sentences short. As a rule, 2 or 3 short sentences will be more effective than a single sentence that goes on forever. Most importantly, don't embed a sentence inside another. When you embed a sentence, like this mini-sentence within a sentence, you're giving the reader too much to absorb at once!

As a rule, a sentence that's 14 words or more will be hard to process, unless...like this...you use a bridge to join the strands together.

## 54. Use numbers - not words

Say '7' rather than 'seven' and you're making the reader's life easier. They can pick out the word with no effort and move onto the next.

## 55. Be Specific

Exact numbers are more believable than rounded or general numbers. So 97 or 103 will carry more weight than 100. Generally, readers will feel the exact number is genuine, while the rounded number feels invented or approximate.

## 56. Keep paragraphs short

A huge block of text will intimidate the average lazy reader. So keep your paragraphs to 4 or 5 lines each - and every now and then, drop in a single line paragraph.

Just to vary the pace.

Like this!

## 57. Break up the copy with sub-headings

Everyone has their own way of reading. Some will read the whole thing, some will glance at the headline and decide to stop or continue...and others will leapfrog through the copy, glancing at the most prominent words to see what's in it for them.

The best way to please the leap froggers is to use sub-headings: mini-headlines that crop up after every 3 or 4 paragraphs to trail the next phase of the message. Each sub-heading should be a compelling statement in its own right, with some teasing copy trailing the news or benefit that's coming.

 When you've written your copy, go back and double-check the sub-headings. If someone just reads the main headline then skips through the sub-headings, will they get a sense of the story? Will they want to go back to the start and read the whole thing?

*Now let's look at the message itself...picking up after the headline:*

## 58. Expand on the headline

Your headline has set an expectation in the reader's mind. You've promised to solve a problem, or fulfil an ambition, or you've lured them in with a teaser. So now they want you to follow it up in your opening paragraph.

This is where so many letters fail. They'll open in a way that feels disconnected from the headline, so readers reach the end of the paragraph and wonder where the message is heading.

For illustration, let's say you're selling last minute places at a business network - so you've written a teasing headline, like this:

# Your Dream Customer Won't Walk Through Your Door Tonight...

## But They Might Walk Through Ours

Then your kicker or sub-heading offers some clarification, like this:

### Join 200 Business Owners at [EVENT NAME] Tonight – only 25 places remain

Now your first paragraph needs to build on the points you've established – like this:

> Tonight, over 200 local business owners - senior decision makers - will meet, swap stories, exchange cards...and lay the foundations for business. But unfortunately, right now, I can't see your name on the list.

This paragraph does two things. Firstly, it re-states the key points: 200 business owners, and the risk of missing out. And secondly, it adds new information: stressing that attendees are senior decision makers, and painting a picture of an informal, productive event.

**That gives the letter a foundation – so from here, it's easy to move into new paragraphs that cover:**

- The type of businesses present

- How the evening works

- Why it's different from other events

- Examples of business done at previous events

- Testimonials from past attendees

- Practical details: where, when, how much and how to book

## 59. Focus on the pain

Once you've drawn the reader in, you can hold their interest by focusing on the pain of living without your solution.

Pain typically comes in two parts:

1. **Frustration,** where you empathise with the reader's situation; then

2. **Agony,** where you turn the screws and show how it affects their life.

For illustration, let's stay with our networking example:

*If the FRUSTRATION is:*
Running a business without influential contacts
*Then the AGONY is:*
Missing out on lucrative contracts, or seeing your competitors getting all the spoils

*If the FRUSTRATION is:*
Wondering where your next customer is coming from
*Then the AGONY is:*
Uncertainty, and living hand to mouth

*If the FRUSTRATION is:*
Ineffective rival networks, where you just meet the same old faces
*Then the AGONY is:*
Feeling stuck in a rut, unable to break free and expand

There's some kind of pain behind every sale. It doesn't matter whether your product helps to solve a problem or fulfil a dream: the pain is always in their current situation – a life without your solution.

# 60. Use an Open Loop

As you get deeper into your message, you have a choice: you can follow a simple, linear path, where one paragraph flows naturally into the next...or you can break up the flow by adding an Open Loop.

The Open Loop is a device used by top copywriters, as a way of forcing essential information onto the reader. This is how it works:

You take the reader to a 'cliffhanger' moment, where you're about to give some juicy information. Then you tell them you'll pick up on that thread shortly, but first you want to explain something else. This gives you a chance to introduce something important, knowing you've got their attention.

This is how we could apply it in our networking letter:

> I don't want you to miss out, so for the next few hours I'm holding you a space. Better yet, I'm also giving you 50% off the entrance fee. And if you claim your place before midday today, there's a special limited bonus..
>
> I'll tell you more about that in a moment.
>
> But first, you're probably wondering why tonight is such a big deal. Well, [....]

From here, you could add some strong sales copy, stressing all the benefits of attending. Or even break off to tell a story about a member who attended and transformed a failing business *(see next point)*. Either way, by the time you 'close the loop' and get back to the enticement, the reader will understand the value of attending.

## 61. Open with a story

In the example we're using here, the letter gets straight to the point – talking about the networking event right from the off.

That's a perfectly valid approach, but it's not the only way. Some of the most successful sales letters in history are built around stories.

Stories work, because they hook us in a way that sales copy can't. They take us on an emotional journey...they trigger our imagination...so we see events played out in our minds, just as we do when we're lost in a novel.

Then of course, when the story ends, we've reached an emotional state – so our minds are primed and ready for the sales message that follows.

So what kind of story should you be telling?

There's no hard and fast rule. It could be about you, or someone you know, or a total stranger. It could be true or invented - it doesn't seem to matter (as long as you don't use the story to make a false claim).

Moreover, your story doesn't have to relate directly to your industry. Like a preacher's sermon, its job is to hold attention and *sow the seeds* for the lesson that follows.

For example, if you sell accounting software, your story doesn't have to be about someone mismanaging their accounts. It could be the tale of someone who left everything until the last minute...then you can relate the tale to your accounting solution.

**Here are 5 ways you can use stories to ease the reader into your letter:**

(1) Describe one person's triumph over adversity

(2) Compare two individuals, and show how one has fared better than the other

(3) Describe the shame or embarrassment of someone who made a bad decision

(4) Describe someone who ignored a problem or opportunity - and paid the price

(5) Show how one key moment turned someone's life around

If you open your letter with a story, come back to it at the end – so you're book-ending the sales message with a story on either side.

At the end, round off the story or draw a lesson from it...a lesson that reminds the reader why they need your solution.

## 62. Describe the features and benefits

Once you've focused the reader on a problem or desire, it's time to set out your stall and introduce your product. Here, the reader wants to know how the product will change their life – so as we covered earlier, it pays to think in terms of benefits over features.

Remember, a feature is what your product does. The corresponding benefit is how that feature helps the customer in a real-life context. Another way to think of this is, "Don't talk about the product...talk about the product of the product: the result it delivers".

**Instant and Ultimate Benefits**
Benefits come in two sizes:

- The Instant Benefit: how the feature makes for a better experience

- The Ultimate Benefit: the knock-on effect that improves the customer's life

Here's an example, for a pro tennis racquet:

**Feature:** professionally strung
**Instant Benefit:** hit with precision
**Ultimate Benefit:** raise your game, be the envy of all challengers

You'll make more impact on the reader if you describe both types of benefit

# 63. Make a bullet list

Bullets work because they help readers to scan the message and pick out the main points. Also, they can be read quickly, because convention says they don't have to be set out as formally as regular text. No-one bats an eyelid if you miss out prepositions and other functional words (at, by, with, from, for, to, etc).

There's no set length for a bullet list. In a 1 or 2 page letter, it could be just a few lines (from 3 to 8 is a safe bet). But in a long form letter, your bullets could easily fill a whole page or more.

When it comes to placement, a bullet list can be used anywhere in your letter. However, it's especially powerful as a way of listing benefits, just before you introduce the offer.

Here are some ways to make your bullets effective:

1.  Add a 'hanger' statement at the top of the list – a simple promise, like "With this product, you'll be able to:"

    Then, make sure every bullet flows from the hanger statement. As in:

    *   [You'll be able to…] Cut down admin time, and spend more time finding new clients

    *   [You'll be able to…] Monitor key tasks, and trigger alerts when deadlines are missed

    *   [You'll be able to…] Track your team's performance, with simple one-click reporting

2.  Start your list with long descriptions of the main benefits – filling 1-2 lines each. Then as you move through the list, start to make your descriptions shorter. Suddenly, the reader is working through the list at a rate of knots, and momentum builds in their mind. This way, you're giving them an adrenalin rush, just before you move in with the offer.

3.  Set every other bullet in bold or a second colour, so the eye can differentiate and skip through the list.

4.  Add a 'Double Punch' Effect: describe the feature first, followed by the Instant Benefit, then Ultimate Benefit.

5.  For variety, invert some of your bullets: describe the benefit before the feature (as in "Do X, thanks to Y").

# 64.  Set your product apart with examples and testimonials

Telling the reader how they'll benefit is not enough. They also want to know why your solution is better than the rest. The problem is, they won't believe you when you hammer home your USP. So you need a third party to say great things on your behalf, and to tell the story of how your product made a difference.

Here are some tips for using examples and testimonials:

• Tackle common objections: think of a reason not to buy, and ask a customer to address it in their story

• Ask customers to give specific details and numbers, to make their story believable

• Use the customer's full name and location - and if you can, add a picture

• In B2B, add the customer's company and job title

101

- Readers are more likely to believe a testimonial or story if it comes from someone reputable, like a doctor or a known and trusted public figure

- Think about flow: if the customer's story helps the flow of the letter, drop it into the main copy. If it spoils the flow, create a box or sidebar and feature it there

- One testimonial is good - but half a dozen will be better!

**Should you re-word testimonials?**

When you're handed a testimonial, it probably won't be word perfect. So what can you do?

You could just use a section that works. Or merge 2 sections, using a....bridge to cut out unusable text.

Failing that, make a few small changes and send it back to the customer for approval. But don't make unauthorised changes, under any circumstances – and if you're rewriting, make sure you don't lose the customer's raw, natural language.

## 65. Back up every claim

We've said it before, the reader wants to believe you. But their brain has a split personality: *The Buyer*, who's ready to go ahead, and *The Sentry* who protects The Buyer from making rash decisions! Every time you make a claim that excites The

Buyer, you trigger The Sentry's natural defences. He wants to see some evidence!

So, be ready to back up your claims – for example:

- Instead of ballpark estimations, give actual numbers.

- Work the details into true-life stories, to add a credible context

- Don't say "studies show" - quote and name the researchers

- Don't say "experts say" – quote and name opinion formers

- Offer safety in numbers, as in "Over 1 million units sold"

**You want to offer proof...but at the same time, you don't want to break the flow of the message. So here's a rule of thumb:**

If it's a small addition, like a number, work it into the main copy. If the detail feels like an overload, try adding it to a sidebar. Or, if it's too 'dry' and dull for a sidebar, set it as a footnote.

## So, you've established the problem and solution - or the ambition and opportunity. So now it's time to move in and get the reader to take action...

## SECTION 7:

# Closing The Deal

**Every letter concludes with a call to action (CTA). It doesn't necessarily mean you're asking the reader for money. The action could be "buy now" or "enquire now", but just as easily it could be "request our free guide" or "visit this web page". It all depends on your reason for sending the mailing.**

One way or another though, you're offering the reader something, and you're asking them to respond. So let's look at that now...

## 66. Set out your offer

You (probably) settled on your offer back in Section 3. Now is the time to make it explicit, with this simple 5-step process:

1) Give your reason for making the offer

2) Set out the main terms of your offer – including the guarantee

3) Stress the deadline and other forms of scarcity, like a limited bonus

4) Repeat the main benefits of taking action now

5) Tell the reader how to respond (by phone, email, post or online) and make it as easy as possible

# 67. Make it exclusive

One of the easiest ways to make your offer more desirable is to tell the reader it's not for everyone.

Talk about the type of person who shouldn't respond: someone who can't afford it, or who won't put it to good use, or expects it to work miracles. Urge those people to stay away, because you only want the best people as customers.

Instantly, the reader sees that you're authentic for turning down business - and they want to see themselves in your group of people with money and goals. Win-win.

As with all things, phrasing is critical here. Some high-end brands come across (by design) as elitist and superior – shamelessly 'shutting out' the lower end of the market. Other brands prefer to be elitist by implication, creating a prestigious feel without explicitly rejecting a section of the market.

You have to decide (or ideally test): which way is right for your brand?

 Take exclusivity a step further, by making readers apply. This tactic is mostly used by coaches and mentors selling personal development products with an element of support. But it could easily be used in other

105

fields. For example, if you're launching a new product, invite readers to be part of a small elite group of early adopters – subject to approval.

## 68. Put your offer price in context

If your offer includes a saving, through a discount or product bundle, be sure to state the regular (higher) price first. This way, the reader will see the offer as a relative saving.

If you position things the other way round - stating the offer price first - it's much harder to see the value.

If you're selling a subscription product, another option is to break down the price into a small daily amount – then compare it with other insignificant daily expenses, like a newspaper or a trip to the coffee shop.

A third option is to liken the product to a non-identical alternative.

For example, if you sell a training manual or DVD, compare it with the trainer's daily consulting rate – telling the reader they can tap into the trainer's expertise for a fraction of the cost of working one-to-one.

## 69. Give a strong Call to Action

When the time comes, you need to tell the reader exactly what to do next – and why. So follow these steps:

106

**Stress the urgency**

Why should the reader respond now? What happens if they delay?

Most marketers build urgency around limited stock, a limited bonus or a time-out offer. This is fine, as long as it's genuine. Consumers are wise to "false scarcity", so there's nothing to gain from faking it!

This is why it helps to give a reason for your offer, as we've already covered. Tell them why you can't make exceptions – then when the time comes, stick to your guns.

**Create a sense of loss**

Immediately after the call to action, remind the reader what life is like without the product. You've shown them all the benefits and painted a bright and rosy future...so now go back to reality and the problem they'll face if they do nothing.

**Handle objections**

You might think it's crazy to put objections in the reader's head! But it's not. The fact is, objections will lurk in their mind whether you address them or not. So if you skirt over them, your response is going to suffer.

But if you get objections out in the open, you're helping the reader to see through the clutter and reach a buying decision. All you have to do is raise the objection...acknowledge it as a valid concern...then use it to show how your product or offer is different from the rest.

To work objections into your letter, try one of these options:

- Raise a major objection in a sub-heading, then tackle it over 2-3 paragraphs.

- Raise a series of objections via a Q&A section, where each question represents a new objection.

- Drop in testimonials where customers talk about their scepticism, and how you overcame their fears.

**Highlight the call to action**

It goes without saying, your call to action should stand out. So try one or more of these highlighting methods:

- Make the text larger

- Make the text a different colour

- Highlight the text in yellow or green

- Add a squiggle, like an asterisk or arrow *(see next section)*

- Set the text in a box or circle

- Add a product or lifestyle shot next to the response mechanism

**Repeat the call to action**

Remember, everyone has their own way of reading. Some will just glance at different parts of the letter, and some will read it without really taking it in. Only a few will read it thoroughly.

So it makes sense to repeat the CTA at least once, to make sure it's noticed and lodged in the reader's mind. Try repeating it below the sign-off, or next to something that will draw the eye like an image or web address.

**How many times should you repeat the CTA?** It depends on how much you need to persuade the reader. If it's a short letter asking for a low-key response, like requesting a free guide, one or two repetitions will do. But if it's a high ticket sale in a long form letter, that number multiplies.

If you're repeating it several times, vary the phrasing here and there. "Call Now" gets boring, so try "We're standing by to help you" or "All it takes is a 2 minute call".

**How do you sell to people after the deadline?** Once the offer has expired, you can't follow up with an offer to extend it – if you did, the reader would never believe you again. But you can make a different offer...a kind of Plan B...that gives people another chance to buy.

For example, if you're selling spaces at a live event, your Plan B offer could be a DVD recording or online access via live streaming. Then you can price the new offer in the same range as the original without compromising your integrity.

## 70. Sign off in blue

Tests have shown that a blue signature increases response. That's probably because a black sig looks photocopied and mass-produced. Blue suggests a level of personal attention.

A good mailing house can make this look even more authentic by printing in a certain blue, layering it in a separate process, or showing imperfections in the way the ink touches the paper.

## 71. Add a P.S.

This is one of the most vital parts of your letter. Readers who scan your copy will head straight for the P.S. because they assume it will give them a concise summary. So don't disappoint. Use the P.S. to repeat the main benefit and offer, plus a reminder of the deadline.

You'll probably find this kind of repetition is more effective than adding new information. Think of it as your last chance to make your pitch.

**"Don't forget" works wonders**
If your P.S. opens with the words "Don't forget" (or "Remember"), you can refer back to some juicy titbit, like a special bonus. Anyone who's scanning the copy will want to know more, so there's a good chance they'll go back and read the letter in full.

**Add credibility below the P.S.**
Chances are you'll have empty space to fill below the P.S. - so don't waste it. Use it to give the reader more reasons to believe. For example:

- Add some customer testimonials - perhaps one that leads with the importance of acting quickly

- Make or repeat your guarantee

- Add some credentials like qualifications, client logos or professional membership badges

# 72. Make full use of the Order Form

If you're enclosing a separate order form, it's as much a part of the sales piece as the main letter. So follow these steps:

**Make your pitch again**
When someone comes to fill in an order form, you have to get them excited for a second time. So make it a mini version of the sales letter, where you repeat the main benefits and add a shot of the product. Also include your phone number and contact details on the form.

**Highlight the main points**
Use colour to highlight product benefits and the big take-aways in the offer, such as:

- Free Delivery

- Limited Stock

- Order before....

- Savings against Recommended Retail Price (RRP)

- Buy 2 and Save £...

**Pre-fill the form**

To make life easier, fill in the reader's name and address, and add any other information like a telephone number or nearest branch. If the form is half-completed, filling in the rest will be less of a chore for the reader.

**Code the form**

When you process the order, you'll want to note where the sale has come from – so add a unique code that matches the mailer's version number. More on measurement in Section 12.

**Allow readers to opt-out from 3rd party mailings**

Through your mailing campaigns, you're going to build a database of buyers - and as this list grows, it will become a valuable asset that you can rent, in part or in whole, to other companies.

If you have tens of thousands of names in your database, this could be a significant source of new revenue.

However, you can only pass on customers' details if they've had the chance to opt out. So it's worth building this in to your campaigns from the start.

All you need is a simple statement like this:

*We may wish to bring you offers from reputable companies*
*– if you prefer not to receive such offers, please tick this box*

Congratulations! You've written a draft letter. Now let's look at how you present it to the reader...

SECTION 8:

# A Matter of Style

Style and layout can make an enormous difference. An average letter that's well laid out can easily out-perform a great letter that's poorly formatted – because the reader will only wade into the copy if it looks inviting.

Let's look at a few ways now to add some visual appeal.

## 73. Alignment makes a difference

Justified text is easier to read than text aligned to the left. It gives your text consistency, which is much easier on the eye than a messy, broken edge.

For best results, you should also add a small indent to the first line of each paragraph, like this. It will help readers to scan the copy and decide if it's worth reading in full.

## 74. Use a serif typeface

Newspapers and books typically use serif fonts, because they're easy to process. Each serif (a small line or stroke at the end of a letter) guides the eye along the page, as an aid to continued reading.

By using the same type of fonts in your mailer, you'll create the same easy read, and add an air of familiarity.

Useful fonts include Times New Roman, Garamond and Imprint MT Std. These are industry standards and often come with software packages including MS Word, so they can be used commercially without a special licence. If you want something different but reliable, you could invest in Adobe Caslon Pro.

While body text is always best served by a serif font, debate still rages over which type works best for headlines and sub-headings. Sans Serif fonts can work well here, perhaps because they're easier to read at a glance. A good compromise option is Optima, which combines the clarity of a sans serif face with the ease of a serif face.

# 75. AVOID BLOCK CAPITALS

READ THIS SENTENCE QUICKLY. IT'S NOT EASY BECAUSE EVERY LETTER IS A CAPITAL. THEY'RE ALL EXACTLY THE SAME HEIGHT, AND THAT MAKES THEM HARDER TO SCAN. ON TOP OF WHICH, IT FEELS LIKE SOMEONE IS SCREAMING AT YOU FROM THE PAGE. READING SHOULD BE A PLEASURE, BUT LIKE THIS IT'S AN UNCOMFORTABLE EXPERIENCE.

Now read this. That's better, isn't it?

The point is, we're not used to reading in block capitals - and anything that makes reading a chore will hurt your response rate.

If you really have to use block capitals, do it SPARINGLY so just one word stands out. But even then, some audiences will find it too "in your face", so think about who you're targeting. In the UK, people who read the red top tabloids will usually accept BLOCK CAPS here and there. But a Daily Mail or broadsheet reader would be more at home with a neater form of emphasis - like *italics*.

Capital letters can be used to good effect in your headline, if you Capitalise The Beginning of Each Word. Look back over the sample headlines given in section 5 and see how many use Initial Caps. This has been extensively tested, and it usually improves response.

For instance, compare:

**Do You Make These Mistakes in Job Interviews?**

With:

**Do you make these mistakes in job interviews?**

The first is more commanding...more deserving of our attention. But note how small words like 'in', 'at' or 'by' are normally set in lower case. Again, this is a proven technique and worth using in your headline.

# 76. Choose paper to suit your market

If you're mailing to a general audience, use a paper stock of 130gsm or better. If you're mailing to a prosperous audience, use a better quality paper. But don't be tempted to use something with a watermark or pattern, because a busy background will take the reader's eye off the message.

# 77. Emphasise key points

You'll want to draw attention to the most important elements on the page. So here are some design features that will help you do it.

Just remember, if you emphasise everything, you emphasise nothing! So do this sparingly...

**Add a squiggle here and there**
'Squiggling' or 'doodling' is a great way to boost response. It means adding handwritten notes in margins or emphasising key words with underlines, boxes, asterisks and more. Squiggles work because they draw the eye, stress the major points and add a human touch to the message.

Just make sure you use squiggles sparingly - and be consistent. They should all be in the same font and colour, so it looks like you've taken a pen and added your notes as an afterthought.

**Add a second colour**
If you're not into squiggles, you can highlight key words by changing the colour. Keep the font either black or dark grey

throughout - bar a few choice words in a striking colour like dark blue, red or purple.

Your second colour is also useful for headlines and sub-headings.

**Consider the psychology of colours**
Different colours carry different meanings – most notably:

- Red says "Treat as urgent"

- Green says "Approved"

- Yellow says "Don't forget, this still needs attention"

- Blue says "trust and authority"

So when you choose a colour for fonts or highlighting, never mind aesthetics - think of the message you want to put across.

**Add a marker effect**
Highlight some key text in yellow or green, so it looks like it's been emphasised with a marker pen. This is a good way to draw attention to a phone number or web address. Alternatively, use it to stress a critical part of the message, like the kicker, offer, or a statement of urgency or scarcity.

# 78. Choose emotive images

The right image can do a lot of the heavy lifting for you. It will draw the reader's eye, lure them in and add some emotional impact. So it's worth investing some time and money to find something that fits - either by arranging a professional photo shoot or searching through an online image library.

Here are some points to consider:

- Generally, pictures of people work better than product or location shots, especially if the subject conveys an emotion like joy or excitement.

- Close-up images work especially well, as they convey the most warmth and emotion.

- If you're selling a product, show someone using it - and enjoying it.

- Pictures of attractive women appeal to both genders and all age groups.

- Make sure your image creates the right impression. Do you want the subject to come across as trustworthy, sympathetic, knowledgeable, relaxed, concerned, elated, confused...or something else entirely?

- If you're hiring a celebrity, they still need to convey the right emotion. A picture of them smiling is all well and good, but does it suit the mood of your letter?

- Many library images are over-used, to the point where readers ignore them. So dig deeper to find something fresh and original.

**Remember Personalisation**

Earlier, we talked about digital printing and how it lets you vary the content of each letter. Well, you can go a long way with variable imagery. People of different genders, ages and social groups will respond to different images, so try segmenting your mailing list into relevant groups.

Oddly, if you're segmenting by age, it pays to show images of people who match your prospects' aspirations - which might not be the age group they belong to!

Broadly speaking, people in their late teens or early 20s will identify with someone who looks slightly older. From their mid 20s to early 40s, they're likely to be happy with images of their own age group. Then from mid 40s onwards, a slightly younger image will make more of an impact.

## 79.   White space doesn't sell...but it lets the message breathe

Most designers will tell you that "white space is essential", while many copywriters will tell you "white space never sold a darn thing"! So where does the truth lie in the big white space debate?

Firstly, it depends on your niche. A busy message, where text and images are crammed in together, might suit loud, aggressive markets like weight loss, fitness and business opportunities. But it's less effective in older, more genteel markets like mobility services or pensions, where a lack of white space is too informal and creates reading problems.

Secondly, consider how much the reader cares about your solution. If you're solving a problem that's costing them money, sleep and sanity, then they'll be ready to wade into the message. White space isn't needed. But if you're trying to convince them they have a problem to start with, they're less inclined to read on - and then white space makes the message feel more accessible.

## 80. Don't end a page on a full stop

As we've said already, a full stop invites you to stop reading. So it can pose a problem every time you get to the end of a page. If a sentence ends at the critical 'PTO' moment, there's a good chance the reader will decide that's enough for now - they've read enough, or they'll put it to one side and carry on later.

The answer is to reach the end of the page mid-sentence - ideally with a cliff-hanger statement like "You'll be left wondering" or "can you manage without"...then the reader can't resist the urge to turn the page.

The mid-sentence page break can be an issue if a letter is written by one person, then typeset by another. The two people need to work together, with the same objective. Then if needed, they can tweak the design or copy to make sure the sentence flows from page to page.

## Letter formatted? Now let's look at the rest of the pack...

SECTION 9:

# The Package

**You've written your letter, and maybe included an order form and envelope. The question now is, how do you flesh out the package? How do you make sure the letter is read, and what other information does the reader need before they can make a decision?**

## 81. Make the most of the envelope

Sometimes a message on the envelope will lift response, and other times it kills it! So treat this with care. It's a good idea to create an envelope that trails the message, and test it against a blank version *(more on testing in section 12)*.

Here are some ways to prepare your envelope

**Add some teaser copy**
Envelope copy is called a 'teaser' for a reason: it's not there to make the sale, just to tease the reader enough to get the letter opened. So try asking a question, or hinting at what's inside - nothing more. If you say too much, the reader will decide they know what it is...and then they'll throw it away without opening.

If your business deals with sensitive topics (especially healthcare), check your industry guidelines on privacy. You may be prohibited from using teaser copy - or even a company logo - as it publicly associates your prospects and customers with your business.

### Tease with a celebrity

If you've hired a celebrity to endorse your mailing, include their image along with your teaser copy or a signed endorsement. If you've chosen your celebrity well, they'll be trusted by your market, so it makes sense to leverage their appeal from the very beginning.

### Personalise the teaser

With variable printing, you can personalise the envelope just the same as the letter. So you could:

- Add the reader's name to the teaser copy – perhaps in a separate, handwritten font.

- Show a picture of a free bonus product, with a shipping label that shows the reader's name.

- Show a lifestyle image of someone who the reader can relate to, using the product.

- Choose an image to suit the reader's passion or outside interests (as already covered), with some short copy that ties the topic into your mailer.

### Test the appearance of your envelope

Envelopes come in all colours, as well as the standard white and manila. They also come in curious shapes - not just the standard DL, C4 and C5. Try a long, slim envelope that fits an A4 sheet folded vertically...if it stands out from the rest of the pile, it's going to be opened.

### Test a window envelope

Window envelopes look official and important, so they often get a higher open rate. Plus, they give you a chance to add some teasing copy just below the final address line...so try making a section of your headline visible inside the window.

### Test a polythene wrapper

If you're enclosing something like a brochure or magazine, a polythene wrapper is a cheap and effective alternative to an envelope. It works because it trails the content, showing there's something of value inside. But as with teaser copy, don't use it if the contents are sensitive.

### Test your logo on the envelope

Again, there's no hard and fast rule here - sometimes your logo will lift response, sometimes it will kill it.

Generally, your logo will help if the reader has requested something from you - for example, if they've requested an information pack through a press advert or your website. It can also help if you already have a good relationship with the reader, or if your brand is well known and generally well thought of. It can be harmful if the reader doesn't know who you are, or has a negative view of your business.

Consider this carefully, and test it to see what works for you.

## 82. Mark the letter as urgent

Using a rubber stamp - or creating one electronically - mark the envelope to add a sense of importance. "Urgent" works well, but you could also try "personal", "private", "confidential", or add more detail like "The information you requested".

Obviously, these statements should never be used to mislead the reader...so don't, for example, suggest they've requested something when they haven't!

## 83. Use a stamp - not a franking machine or PPI

Nothing screams "bulk mailing" more than the mark of a franking machine or a Postage Paid Impression (PPI). So add a real stamp - and for a special touch, try positioning it slightly askew. It tells the reader "this has been sent by a human being"!

Of course, real stamps are more expensive than the bulk postage options. However, it could make the difference between getting read and getting binned. What's more, if you send 4000 pieces or more and get your mailing house to pre-sort the order, you'll qualify for a sorted mail discount...and then there's a trick of the trade that can offset the price increase.

All you have to do is stamp, sort and mail the letters - then your mailing house will pre-cancel the stamps. The mailing is then dispatched and you can claim back the difference between the cost of the stamps and the bulk sorted price.

Your mailing house should be able to manage this for you. Yes, it costs more money but if it increases your responses – which it may well do – it is all about the final result, not simply the cost of production.

**Reduce your postage costs**

While cost should be far less important to you than ROI, you'll still want to keep your postage bill to a minimum. Here are some ways to achieve this in the UK:

- As above, pre-sort and mail at least 4000 pieces.

- Keep your package below 100 grams - unless you have good reason to go over.

- If you can, use DL or C5 envelopes – they cost much less than the larger alternatives.

- Use quality data that can be verified against the Royal Mail Postal Addressed File (PAF).

- Use a machine readable font to eliminate sorting queries.

- Allow 3- 4 days for delivery. Then you can use Economy Mail or a Downstream Access provider like Whistl or Secured Mail.

# 84. Add a lift item

You're paying for postage anyway, so you might as well fill the envelope up to 100 grams. So first, weigh the package and see much room is left - if any. If you have space, and you've already included an envelope and order form, what can you add as a "lift item": an extra insert to help the customer decide?

**How about...?**

- A case study, with a testimonial from a happy customer

- A full list of features and benefits

- A comparison chart, showing how your product beats the competition

- A detailed summary of your free report or other giveaway

- Your guarantee, formatted as a certificate

- A cheque offering money back

- A voucher or flyer, offering a bonus or special deal

- A letter of endorsement from a customer, patron or public figure

- The science bit: clinical proof that your product meets industry standards

- A postcard repeating the main proposition and call to action

- A trailer for a web page where they can find out more and sign up online

Whatever you insert, make sure it complements the package. There's no sense throwing in just anything, just to make up the weight! If it doesn't add to the proposition, it's got no business being there.

For that reason, you should think carefully before enclosing something generic like a catalogue, brochure, or anything else that diverts the reader's attention. Generic pieces can work, of course, if your mailer is focused on a range of services...but generally, direct mail works best when you make a specific offer and support it with relevant inserts.

## 85. Add something lumpy!

Direct marketers have had a lot of success simply by enclosing random bits and pieces, as a way of adding a touch of curiosity. Items are usually the size and value of a Christmas cracker toy, so they don't cost much to buy or post. But they make the package lumpy, increasing the reader's curiosity - and as a result, getting more letters opened and read.

The item should then be used as a jumping off point for the letter. For example, you could enclose a whistle and say "Use this whenever you need me". Or enclose an egg timer and say "Time is running out".

It's a tongue-in-cheek way to grab attention - so if you do this, your letter should be just as light-hearted.

 Your lumpy insert doesn't have to tie in to the letter! We've seen one example where an elastic band was added to the pack. It had nothing to do with the mailing at all, and yet it increased response.

## 86. Buy the reader's attention

As an alternative to adding random lumpy items, try sending something that makes the reader feel obliged to give their attention.

It could be something as simple as a teabag or coffee sachet, with a note saying "put the kettle on and take 5 minutes to read this". Or in B2b, maybe a 10p coin for the coffee machine?

Be careful what you send though, because it has to go through the post. Food items, no matter how innocent, can be the most problematic. Remember, chocolate melts, biscuits get crushed and nuts can trigger allergies...so choose carefully.

A lottery ticket is a great way to buy attention, but only in the right circumstances. It's not wise for mass mailings, because costs will be too high. And it shouldn't be used if you're mailing to staff – especially in public sector - because there are many rules around accepting gifts. But if you're mailing to a highly qualified list of business owners, it's a sound device because it can't possibly be ignored. Plus, for most people it invokes the law of reciprocity: you've given something valuable, so they feel obliged to give their attention in return.

## 87. Create a shock and awe effect

If you've identified high value prospects, maybe you can afford to spend more reeling them in. So let your imagination loose and think of something outlandish. For example:

- Have the letter hand-delivered by a singing telegram

- Buy ad space on a nearby billboard, and use it to trail the letter

- Send the letter by courier, and make the reader sign for it

- Send a pay-as-you-go mobile phone, with your number programmed in

- Send an MP3 player, pre-loaded with a personal message from you

- Offer tickets to a major event, in exchange for visiting a web page

- Attach the letter to a waste paper basket, inviting the reader to throw it away

Obviously, this type of mailing can bankrupt you in next to no time! So test it on a very small scale and see how people respond...then weigh up the value of their business against the cost. Do the numbers stack up?

**Finally, the whole package is finished! So next, let's check it's ready to go...**

SECTION:10

# The Final Appraisal

We've covered a lot of bases, but don't panic - it's impossible to use every point in every campaign. So now, as you review your package, let's simplify things a little. What should you be looking for before you give the green light?

## 88. Follow the 4-part checklist

Maxwell Sackheim was the founder of the Book-of-the-Month Club - the first ever direct-mail book club in the United States. Every time Max created or reviewed a letter, he used these 4 questions as a guide:

### 1. Why should anyone read or listen to this?

*In other words, does your offer match your target market...and have you done enough to grab and hold their attention?*

### 2. Why should anyone believe it?

*Have you added trust and credibility elements, like a reason for the offer, testimonials or mini case studies?*

133

**3. Why should anyone do anything about it?**

*Are you giving readers something they want...or at least, something they need? If it's need based, does the copy emotively change the need to a want?*

**4. Why should it be acted upon immediately?**

*What's the urgency? Are you stressing limited stock, a limited bonus or a time-out offer...or showing the reader why they shouldn't live another day without you?*

# 89. Check for comprehension

If your package passes the checklist, find a guinea pig - someone who matches your target market - and ask them to check through it before you send it out. Ask them if it makes sense, and get them to repeat the main points back to you. If they've misunderstood anything, take another look...then check back with them until they're happy that it all makes sense.

Be careful who you select as your guinea pig. Ask your partner, your family, your friends by all means but recognise they may be biased towards your business - and worse, they may not have any empathy with your customers.

If you can, find someone neutral who matches your ideal customer's demographics and interests.

# 90. Check for impact

Your guinea pig should be able to tell you if the package hits home, and pick out any elements that would turn them off.

Be sure to ask them about:

- Your style of language, and specific words they love or hate.

- The emotional angle: are you hitting the mark?

- The offer - is it suitable and compelling? (Would it make them buy or at least consider buying?)

- The envelope: does it turn them off, or make them want to know more?

- The inserts: do they add to the call to action, or confuse it?

- The missing link: what's stopping them from responding...and what should be in the package to get them past the line?

Your guinea pig's feedback matters, but only up to a point. Insightful as this process might be, it only gives you an opinion. If you want to know for sure, you have to pitch it to the market.

So, the worst thing you could do is change every last thing that the guinea pig objects to.

Just get their general reaction to the main points above...change any major issues...then let the market decide.

Once you have some real data to work with, you can re-visit their notes and consider smaller changes.

---

**That's it – the job is done. You're ready to send your first mailer...then start the process of continuous improvement.**

SECTION:11

# Testing & Measuring

**No matter how good your letter is, it can be improved. A tweak here and there can have a surprising impact on your results...but first, you have to know what to change, and why.**

**So where do you start?**

The answer lies in testing and measurement. That means throwing something out there to see how the market responds, then testing new ideas to see if they make a difference.

The good news for you is, most UK companies see testing as a luxury!

Typically, they'll look at the first set of results and draw instant conclusions. If it works, they'll let it run without trying to improve - and if it fails, they'll assume the whole concept is flawed and cast it aside.

Those who bother to test and measure will always have more success. So here, we'll go through the basic steps you'll need to put in place...

## 91. Start with a simple A/B test

Split your prospect base into two equal groups (Group 1 and Group 2) making sure the data is equally split across your geographical area.

Then create two letters (Version A and Version B), sending A to Group 1 and B to Group 2.

Make sure each letter is coded so that you know where every response has come from.

When you create your A/B versions, you have two options: Micro Variation or Radical Variation.

**Micro Variation** means there's only one difference between Versions A and B. That could be a different headline, offer or call to action – or anything else, as long as you stick to one single (but significant) change.

This is a good choice if you're confident in your approach – for example, if you're building on previous successful campaigns.

**Radical Variation** means the two versions are totally different. That could mean testing a long letter versus a short letter, a letter versus a postcard, or writing from two different angles.

This is a good choice if you're torn between two approaches – most likely, if you have no precedents to learn from.

**Test a reliable volume**

A test that uses 1,000 prospects is a good start for a very small business. But quite obviously, a larger test is far more reliable. To gain solid results, your volume should be up to 10 times higher - so ideally, you'd mail two batches of 5,000 each.

# 92. Test again...or appoint a 'Control' piece

When you mail your first test versions, keep a close eye on responses.

If both versions get zero response, you should go back to the drawing board and test something new. This is painful, because you won't know why the campaign failed. You'll have to rely on instinct, and any feedback you've received – ideally from customers or your own sales people.

However, in the more likely event that you get some response, you should find that one version has out-performed the other - even if the difference is very slight.

That gives you something to build on.

Your winning version is now your 'Control' – the marketing equivalent of a reigning boxing champion! Now every time you mail, you can send the Control and trial it head to head against a 'Test' or 'Challenger'. If the Test brings in the best results, it becomes the new Control.

**Once you've established a Control, forget Radical Variation**

Your goal now is continuous improvement, and you can only achieve that through Micro Variation: systematically testing one small change after another.

## 93. Work towards the ultimate version

Your early tests should focus on the major elements of your mailer – including:

- Headline
- Pricing
- Offer
- Bonuses
- Opening paragraph
- Body copy
- Bullet lists

- Call to action
- Testimonials
- Response mechanism
- Envelope teaser copy
- Layout
- Lifestyle images
- Product images

Approach these elements one by one – for example, if you're mailing once a week, spend the first few months of the campaign testing different headlines.

Once you've found a headline that keeps on winning, move on and start testing different price points...then different offers...and so on.

Crucially, you should establish firm controls around each major element before you start testing the more incidental elements – including:

- Picture captions
- Colour scheme
- Font
- Envelope style

- Envelope colour
- Inserts
- Highlighting
- Squiggles

**Never stop testing**

As the process continues, you'll find it gets harder and harder to beat your Control. But that doesn't mean you've found the ultimate version. Keep on testing. In the past, successful Controls have run month after month for decades...but eventually they've been beaten. And often, just one small change has made a major difference.

# 94. Think before you replace your Controls

When you run your first A/B test, the difference between response rates doesn't really matter. It could be microscopic - as long as one version beats the other, you've got a reason to declare a winner and move forward with a Control piece.

BUT - once you've got a Control in place, don't replace it without good reason. If a Test only beats it by a fraction, you should weigh things up before you accept that the Control has been beaten.

For example, could there be a blip caused by geography or timing? Or does common sense tell you that the difference is only 1 or 2 sales, so the uplift is only a matter of coincidence? If you're in doubt, don't be a slave to the data - run the test again, and again until you're happy to appoint the Test as your new Control.

## 95. Test Multi-Media

There's one test you can run without making a single change to the mailer. Send your control piece out in two regions - and in one, create a backdrop of awareness through multi-media channels. That could mean advertising via local TV, radio, press or billboards...regionally-targeted display ads on popular websites...appearances at trade shows or in retail concessions...or if you have the data, using e-mail or SMS messaging.

You'll probably find that when you combine DM with at least one other channel, your mailer delivers a better response - even if the other media channels make little or no direct contribution.

## 96. Code Everything

As mentioned, you need to code each version of your letter so you can track responses and run your A/B tests. To do this efficiently, you should set up a spreadsheet that shows the code of each version, the numbers and dates of each mailing, and the results in terms of either leads, sales or revenue.

In the same folder, keep a digital sample of each version for future reference.

Then, you need to make sure codes can be tracked. You can do that by:

**EITHER**...Setting up a unique telephone number or web address for each version.

**AND/OR**...Using the code as an offer code, placed next to the call to action, so responders can quote it over the phone or on a web page.

**AND/OR**...Adding the code to returnable items, like an order form or pre-paid envelope.

Then of course, make sure staff are trained to record every important detail!

So far, so good.

But this only records results at the top level – at version level. Your records will tell you which versions win and lose, but they won't tell you why!

That's because, over time, you'll be testing a number of key elements like the headline, layout, offer, deadline, call to action and more – as well as external factors, like the source of your list, target segments, campaign timing and competitive trends.

Top level coding won't show you which of these elements win and lose. So you'd be constantly digging out old versions, comparing them side by side and making off-the-cuff judgements that could send you off in the wrong direction.

To make life easier, you should code each element individually – just something simple like Headline 1, Headline 2 and Headline 3. Then, in your spreadsheet, note which version contains which element codes.

This way, when you view results, you can see instantly which headline works, which layout works, which offer works and more. It's clinical, indisputable data that you can access instantly – helping you to edge closer to the ultimate version of your letter.

In time, this process will eliminate guesswork altogether, and take you to a point where success is predictable – and inevitable.

## 97. Fail Fast and Move on…

You've probably heard of Thomas Edison's philosophy, to celebrate every failure. When he was inventing the lightbulb, he knew that every failed experiment brought him one step closer to finding the method that worked.

Well, every direct marketer needs to take a lead from Edison's book. You'll have successes and failures, and they're both instructive – helping you to understand what pushes the customer's buttons, and taking you ever closer to the ultimate version of your mailer.

So, treat every failure as a lesson learned. Of course, doing this requires some discipline. So...

**Keep good records**

Set up a campaign log, including archive mailers and a spreadsheet of results.

As a minimum, you should record:

- The date of each mailing

- A code for each version mailed

- Number of records mailed

- Postcodes mailed

- Segments mailed - including demographics, interest groups or types of business

- Response Rates

- Conclusions drawn from testing

- Conversion of leads to sales

Compiling these records guarantees that lessons are never forgotten, and new members of your team have an easy point of reference.

You need your call centre, order processing and website monitoring teams to supply reliable data.

Don't assume everyone will complete the code when ordering – some will forget, and others might decide it's unimportant!

If you want accurate results, you have to stay on top of this process.

### Spot the Patterns of Success

Update your results daily and before long, you'll know the pattern of a successful campaign.

You'll know what percentage of responses come in within a given timeframe - so within a few days of a new mailer hitting, you should be able to predict final numbers.

If the mailer is a hit, this allows you to plan your resources – such as rolling out more mailings, or adding capacity in your fulfilment or support team.

And if it fails, at least you'll know sooner rather than later. You can draw conclusions and move on to the next test, instead of waiting until the end of a promotional period.

## 98. Mail again…and again

Most marketers give up too soon. They'll assume that a customer who fails to respond is saying no. While in reality, some won't even see or open the mailer...some will read it with interest, but get distracted before responding...some will think the time is wrong...and only the final few will decide it's definitely not for them.

So don't stop mailing. As long as you're making money each time you send it, carry on. That means sending a follow-up mailer as your deadline approaches, and re-sending the original mailer every few months.

Eventually of course, your responses will start to dip, so you'll need to buy in more data and saturate the new list. But even then, your original list shouldn't be put out to pasture. Try mailing a little less often, or sending a different offer. You can still profit.

## 99. Test different days and seasons

There's no generic evidence to favour a certain day of the week for mailing. But in your business, you might find there is an optimum day. So try mailing at different times of the week to see if there's a pattern.

If you sell consumer products, start by testing towards the end of the week, because people start to think more about their personal lives as the weekend approaches. If you sell to businesses, the early part of the week is more likely to work for you – although Mondays might be a bad choice, because many senior figures will tell you it's their busiest day.

You'll also find that certain months or seasons are better than others. In the past, July and August were likely to cause a lull, but that doesn't seem to happen anymore. The only month to approach with caution is December – even if you tie your promotion into the festive season, you're competing for attention like never before.

Naturally though, seasons vary from one product to the next. For example, self-improvement products perform best in January and September, while in-home entertainment products are especially popular through autumn and winter.

**What's happening in the world...and will it make a difference?**

Sometimes, an event or happening can impact on response – sometimes in a good way, sometimes bad.

Take the weather. If you're mailing to sell holidays and there's a sudden heat wave, your response will dip. But if the same mailer hits at a time of severe rainfall, response will go up.

In the same way, current news and events can make a difference. If you're raising money for a small local charity and a global disaster strikes, people will choose to give their money to the more urgent cause. But if you happen to mail at a time when your cause ties into a news story, there's no question that you'll see a better response.

Often of course, there's nothing you can do about this. Weather and news are uncontrollable, so it's largely down to good or bad luck.

However, there are some ways of controlling the chaos. Long-term forecasts will tell you if extreme weather is likely. Some news stories will build up quietly before they make the headlines. And major events are scheduled, so you know when they'll come around.

**So, if you feel that events have the power to change your response, look ahead as far as you can...and if time permits, reschedule.**

# 100. Scale up!

Once you've developed a winning mailer, you can start to mail more pieces and expect to see the same results on a bigger scale. So if 10,000 pieces gets you 400 orders, 50,000 should bring you 2,000 orders – or thereabouts.

The bigger the data set, the more accurately you can predict your result. So you might want to phase your testing to limit the leap from test to rollout. For example, move from 10,000 to 20,000, then to 35,000 before the full rollout of 50,000.

Whatever the numbers, of course, this will never be an exact science. But as a rule, patterns tend to repeat plus or minus a few per cent. So you can proceed with confidence, knowing you've taken away the guesswork.

**However, patterns only repeat when your scaled-up campaign mirrors the conditions of the test campaign. That means:**

- The list is profiled the same way - no other customer types are added in, just to make up the numbers.

- Your target customers still have the same problem, and the same range of alternative solutions.

- The message, offer and response mechanism are identical.

- The deadline gives the prospect the same amount of time to respond.

- Your brand still has the same reputation and level of awareness.

# 101. Buy in more data – and target rapid expansion

You've mailed to a certain type of audience, and the mailer worked. So now talk to a list broker and find more of the same.

There's an easy way to do this, by applying the same criteria on a larger scale. But there's also a smarter way - by taking a closer look at the people who responded, and finding people who match their profile for the next campaign.

For example, maybe all your respondents work in the same industry? Or share a common interest? Or live in the same region? Take a look at every characteristic, from age groups and demographics right through to media preferences...just the same as you did at the very start of the process...and if there's a common theme, build up a 'Hyper Responsive' list of similar people.

There are millions of records out there. In the 21st Century, high quality data is available on virtually everyone, so a well-tested mailer can easily be expanded - and rapidly become a profitable full-scale campaign.

This is what differentiates direct mail from e-mail marketing.

# And finally...be a willing investor

This is not about creating the cheapest mailing piece – it's about maximising your Return On Investment.

It's very rare that the cheapest campaign brings in the highest response. So be ready to invest and work through the process of testing, failing and learning.

In the end, you'll have a scalable, predictable source of business. And by then, we're sure you'll agree, it's been worth the effort!

## APPENDIX

# Successful Sales Letters

Over the next few pages, we've shared a small number of classic and lesser-known sales letters. We've deliberately chosen a diverse mix, to show different writing styles, layouts and types of proposition.

The only thing they have in common is that they've all succeeded by staying true to the established principles that we've covered in this book.

*The Wall Street Journal Letter 1 - The most successful direct marketing piece in history*

## THE WALL STREET JOURNAL,
### World Financial Center, 200 Liberty Street, New York, NY 10281

Dear Reader:

On a beautiful late spring afternoon, twenty-five years ago, two young men graduated from the same college. They were very much alike, these two young men. Both had been better than average students, both were personable and both—as young college graduates are—were filled with ambitious dreams for the future.

Recently, these men returned to their college for their 25th reunion.

They were still very much alike. Both were happily married. Both had three children. And both, it turned out, had gone to work for the same Midwestern manufacturing company after graduation, and were still there.

But there was a difference. One of the men was manager of a small department of that company. The other was its president.

### What Made The Difference

Have you ever wondered, as I have, what makes this kind of difference in people's lives? It isn't a native intelligence or talent or dedication. It isn't that one person wants success and the other doesn't.

The difference lies in what each person knows and how he or she makes use of that knowledge.

And that is why I am writing to you and to people like you about The Wall Street Journal. For that is the whole purpose of The Journal: to give its readers knowledge—knowledge that they can use in business.

### A Publication Unlike Any Other

You see, The Wall Street Journal is a unique publication. It's the country's only national business daily. Each business day, it is put together by the world's largest staff of business-news experts.

Each business day, The Journal's pages include a broad range of information of interest and significance to business-minded people, no matter where it comes from. Not just stocks and finance, but anything and everything in the whole, fast-moving world of business … The Wall Street Journal gives you all the business news you need—when you need it.

### Knowledge Is Power

Right now, I am reading page one of The Journal, the best-read front page in America. It combines all the important news of the day with in-depth feature reporting. Every phase of business news is covered, from articles on inflation, wholesale prices, car prices, tax incentives for industries to major developments in Washington, and elsewhere. (over, please)

And there is page after page inside The Journal, filled with fascinating and significant information that's useful to you. The

*The Wall Street Journal Letter 1 - The most successful direct marketing piece in history*

Marketplace section gives you insights into how consumers are thinking
and spending. How companies compete for market share. There is daily
coverage of law, technology, media and marketing. Plus daily features
on the challenges of managing smaller companies.

The Journal is also the single best source for news and statistics
about your money. In the Money & Investing section there are helpful
charts, easy-to-scan market quotations, plus "Abreast of the Market,"
"Heard on the Street" and "Your Money Matters," three of America's most
influential and carefully read investment columns.

If you have never read The Wall Street Journal, you cannot imagine how
useful it can be to you.

### A 13 Week Subscription
Put our statements to the proof by subscribing for the next 13 weeks
for just $34. This is the shortest subscription term we offer—and a
perfect way to get acquainted with The Journal. Or you may prefer to
take advantage of our better buy-one year for $129.

Simply fill out the enclosed order card and mail it in the postage-paid
envelope provided. And here's The Journal's guarantee: should The
Journal not measure up to your expectations, you may cancel this
arrangement at any point and receive a refund for the undelivered
portion of your subscription.

If you feel as we do that this is a fair and reasonable proposition,
then you will want to find out without delay if The Wall Street Journal
can do for you what it is doing for millions of readers. So please mail
the enclosed order card now, and we will start serving you immediately.

About those two college classmates I mention at the beginning of this
letter: they were graduated from college together and together got
started in the business world. So what made their lives in business
different?

Knowledge. Useful knowledge. And its application.

### An Investment In Success
I cannot promise you that success will be instantly yours if you start
reading The Wall Street Journal. But I can guarantee that you will find
The Journal always interesting, always reliable, and always useful.

Sincerely,
/s/ Peter R. Kann

Peter R. Kann
Publisher

PRK:er
Encs.

P.S. It's important to note that The Journal's subscription price may
be tax deductible. Ask your tax advisor.

*The Wall Street Journal Letter 2 - The 2nd letter that finally beat the original - after 28 years of testing*

# THE WALL STREET JOURNAL.

WORLD FINANCIAL CENTER, 200 LIBERTY STREET, NEW YORK, NY 10281

Dear Reader:

On a beautiful late spring afternoon, twenty-five years ago, two young men graduated from the same college.

They were very much alike, these two young men. Both had been better than average students, both were personable and -- as young college graduates are -- both were filled with ambitious dreams for the future.

Recently, these men returned to their college for their twenty-fifth reunion.

They were still very much alike.  Both were happily married.  Both had children.  And both, it turned out, had gone to work for the same Midwestern company after graduation, and were still there.

But there was a difference.  One of the men was manager of a small department of that company.  The other was its president.

#### What made the difference

Have you ever wondered, as I have, what makes this kind of a difference in people's lives?  It isn't native intelligence or talent or dedication. It isn't that one person wants success and the other doesn't.

The difference lies in what each person knows and how he or she uses that knowledge.

And that's why I'm writing to you about The Wall Street Journal.  For the whole purpose of the Journal is to give its readers knowledge -- advantageous knowledge they can use in business.

(over, please)

*The Wall Street Journal Letter 2 - The 2nd letter that finally beat the original - after 28 years of testing*

---

Just recently, The Wall Street Journal made the biggest changes in it's 113-year history –– to make it easier for you to access this special knowledge. We've added color and made design improvements in every section and, as a result, today's Journal is fresher, more reader-friendly –– and more useful to you, more quickly. The day's vital stories stand out to help you select those that interest you.

### The best-read front page in America

Right now, I'm looking at page one of the Journal, the best-read front page in America. The excellent layout is unchanged, but it's a faster read. It combines all the important news of the day with in-depth reporting. Every phase of business news is covered -- business forecasts, breaking stories, politics -- stories from Washington, Moscow, Frankfurt, Tokyo -- item after item that could affect you, your job, your future.

Now, if you're jammed for time, a 10-minute scan will set you up for the day.

### An improved Wall Street Journal and "the business of life"

More than just business, the world's most trusted source of business news and information has also added <u>Personal Journal</u>, a major new section appearing every Tuesday through Thursday. It taps the world's largest staff of business news experts for information of per- sonal benefit to you. Not only personal investing and personal technology, but careers, health and fitness, family, and everything about <u>the business of life</u>.

### The battle for the consumer

<u>Marketplace</u> gives you revealing insights into how consumers are thinking and spending -- and how compa- nies are competing for market share. Plus coverage of law, media, technology, marketing, and the challenges of managing smaller companies.

### "...the best source for news...about your money"

Today's Journal is also the single best source for news and statistics about your money. In the

*The Wall Street Journal Letter 2 - The 2nd letter that finally beat the original - after 28 years of testing*

Money & Investing section, there are helpful charts, now even easier to grasp in color -- and three of America's most carefully scrutinized and influential investment columns -- "Abreast of the Market," "Heard on the Street," and "Your Money Matters."

So, every section, column and feature that contributes to making today's Journal the final authority in business news is right there, where it's always been -- with two major additions: A new section, Personal Journal, that's all about "the business of life"-- and design changes to make the Journal easier to use and more useful to you.

For business news, today's Journal is the only newspaper you need

And Weekend Journal wraps up the week on Fridays with wise and witty reviews of the arts and entertainment, sports, travel, country life, and fun-filled ways to spend your hard-earned free time.

No matter how many times you've seen The Wall Street Journal, I urge you to take a fresh look at today's Journal. It's the talk of the business world. For business, it's the only newspaper you need.

Your own personal subscription

Put us to the test: Subscribe for 26 weeks for only $89. (You save $38 off the newsstand price.)

Or take advantage of our better buy: 52 weeks for $175 -- and save $79! Either way, you pay nothing extra for home or office delivery every business day.

While I cannot promise you instant

success if you subscribe, I guarantee that you will
find The Wall Street Journal consistently interesting,
totally reliable, and always useful.

                        Our guarantee to you

     Should The Wall Street Journal not measure up to
your expectations, or to anything I've said, you may
cancel your subscription at any time and receive a full
refund for the undelivered portion.

     If you feel that this is fair and reasonable,
you'll want to find out promptly if The Wall Street
Journal can do for you what it has done for millions of
readers.  So, order your subscription today and we'll
start serving you immediately.

                         Sincerely,



                         Peter R. Kann, Publisher
PRK:md
Encs.

P.S.  About those two college classmates I mentioned at
      the beginning of this letter:  They graduated
      from college together and got started in business
      together.  So what made their success in business
      different?  Knowledge.  Useful knowledge.  And
      its application.

*The Letter that built American Express - Simple, benefit-heavy copy that started an empire*

# The letter that built American Express

Dear Mr. Smith:

Quite frankly, the American Express Card is not for everyone. And not everyone who applies for Card membership is approved.

However, because we believe you will benefit from Card Membership, I've enclosed a special invitation for you to apply for the most honored and prestigious financial instrument available to people who travel, vacation, and entertain.

The American Express Card is the perfect example of the old adage, "You get what you pay for."

For example, you get a truly impressive array of extra privileges, all designed for your convenience and security:

- A Worldwide Network of Travel Service Offices* is at your Service. Enjoy personal attention at any of the nearby 1,000 American Express Offices -- Your "homes away from home" -- around the globe.

- Cash your Personal Check at Thousands of Locations. Cash up to $250 at participating hotels and motels, and up to $1,000 at most American Express Travel Services Offices all over the world. (Subject to cash availability and local regulations.)

- Card Lost or Stolen? You'll Get a Quick Replacement. If the Card is lost or stolen, an emergency replacement will be provided at any Travel Service Office in the world, usually by the end of the next business day.

- Obtain Emergency Funds Instantly. Once you've enrolled in this convenient service, our network of automated Travelers Cheque Dispensers lets you obtain up to $500 ... in 60 seconds or less!

- Carry $100,000 of Travel Accident Insurance. Just charge your tickets to the Card, and you, your spouseor dependent children under the age of 23 are automatically covered when traveling by common carrier on land, sea, or in the air. It's underwritten by Fireman's Fund Insurance Companies, San Rafael, California, for approximately 35 cents of the annual Card Membership fee.

- Your Hotel Reservations are Assured. As an American Express Card Member, if you request, your hotel room will be held for you until checkout the following day at nearly 8,000 participating hotels.

- Enjoy Special Express Hotel Service. Speedy check-in and checkout is available to Card Members at more than 1,000 hotels, including Hilton, Hyatt, Marriott, Sheraton, and more.

Extras like these only begin to tell the story of American Express Card security, emergency protection, and convenience. You'll also enjoy:

*The Letter that built American Express - Simple, benefit-heavy copy that started an empire*

- Unequalled Mobility. The Card is welcomed by the world's major airlines, car rental agencies, railroads, and cruise lines. Plus it pays for auto parts and servicing at thousands of locations nationwide.

- A Worldwide Welcome. Fine restaurants, hotel resorts, and a host of other establishments around this world, and right in your hometown, recognize the Card and welcome your patronage.

- Purchasing Power. No need to carry large amounts of cash. The Card takes care of shopping needs, whether you're choosing a wardrobe, buying theater tickets, sending flowers, or hosting a dinner (even if you can't be there!)

- Financial Freedom. Unlike bank cards, the American Express Card imposes no pre-set spending limit. Purchases are approved based on your ability to pay as demonstrated by your past spending, payment patterns, and personal resources. So you are free to make your own decisions about when and where to use the Card.

In a few words, American Express Card Membership is the most effective letter of introduction to the world of travel, entertainment, and the good life yet devised. Yet surprisingly, these benefits are all yours to enjoy for the modest fee of just $35 a year.

Why not apply for Card Membership today? All you have to do is fill out and mail the enclosed application. As soon as it is approved, we'll send along the Card, without delay.

Sincerely,

Diane Shalb
Vice President

P.S.    Apply today, and enjoy all the benefits of Card Membership. Those listed here are just a handful of what's available. A full listing is included in the Guide to Card Member Services you'll receive along with the Card.

*The Bowery Mission - A charity appeal with inserts and strong copy cosmetics*

Tuesday morning

Dear Friend,

$1.59 doesn't buy much these days.

But there is a place -- The Bowery Mission -- where $1.59 can provide a complete Thanksgiving meal. And help a homeless man or woman find hope and new life.

My name is Ed Morgan. I'm the president at the Mission. For 130 years, we've been reaching out to New York's hungry and hurting with love and compassion -- providing food, shelter and life-changing programs.

Rising unemployment and rising utility bills are hurting thousands of struggling men and women in our community. Many of them end up at The Bowery Mission -- broken and confused -- because they simply have nowhere else to go.

This Thanksgiving, hundreds of desperate people will pour into our Mission. Some of them will be young men unable to find work -- frightened and homeless for the very first time. Feeding them is the first step. Once this immediate need has been met, we offer job-skills training that can help qualify them for employment.

Then there are the older ones, worn out and weary from years on the streets. They've tried many times to pick themselves up -- and failed. For them, hope begins with a friendly face and an understanding heart at the Mission.

Others have spent their lives running from problems -- often by abusing drugs or alcohol. When they realize running won't help, we're here to offer them recovery and rehabilitation programs that can guide them toward a more productive life.

And then there are the families. **Most are single moms with young children.** Life has been cruel to them -- filled with fear, loneliness and oftentimes abuse. What does it mean

(over, please)

*The Bowery Mission - A charity appeal with inserts and strong copy cosmetics*

to them to be able to enjoy a hot, nutritious meal in safe surroundings?  It means everything!

A hearty, traditional Thanksgiving meal at The Bowery Mission can be the first step to getting each of these individuals back on their feet and off the streets -- and helping them become productive, hardworking members of our community.

Every time we help a broken, lost man or woman put their life back together, we improve the quality of life in New York.  That's why I'm asking you to help them take that first step this Thanksgiving -- by helping to provide them with hot, nutritious holiday meals.

Because each meal costs just $1.59, your gift will go further than you may have thought possible.  For example, a gift of $19.08 will help provide 12 people with a Thanksgiving meal and other care.  A gift of $34.98 will help feed and care for 22 people.  And $54.06 will make it possible for 34 homeless and hungry people to enjoy a traditional Thanksgiving meal -- and perhaps start them on the road to a new life.

It begins when you return the enclosed meal ticket with your check for one of the amounts shown.

As you sit down to your own Thanksgiving feast, you'll have the satisfaction of knowing your spare change has been turned into "life change" -- giving hope and new life to homeless people right here in New York.  Thank you so much.

Happy Thanksgiving to you and your family!

Sincerely,

Ed Morgan
President

P.S. With more and more people turning to us every day for food and shelter, it's vitally important that we be fully prepared for the Thanksgiving rush.  Please help us by sending your gift today.

*-- or by Wednesday, November 25th at the latest!*

*The Bowery Mission - A charity appeal with inserts and strong copy cosmetics*

**Our Pledge of Accountability**

At The Bowery Mission, we trust God to provide the various resources we need to help the homeless, hungry and hurting of our great city. We are eternally grateful to those individuals who have acted in their desire to share their love for the needy by partnering financially in our ministry.

**We are committed to:**

- Using your contributions faithfully and wisely, in accordance with our mission to minister in New York City to men, women and children caught in cycles of poverty, hopelessness and dependencies of many kinds, and to see their lives transformed to hope, joy, lasting productivity and eternal life through the power of Jesus
- Respecting your privacy, by refusing to make your name, address or any other personal information available to any other entity
- Contracting with an independent accounting firm to conduct an annual

audit of our finances, and making our financial reports available to all who request them.

On occasion, we receive more contributions for a given project than are needed. When this happens, we use the funds to meet a similar pressing need. If for any reason you feel that our Board of Directors and administrative staff have mismanaged your contribution to our organization, please contact us for a refund equal to the total amount of your gift.

**Your gift provides more than a meal!**

On average, it costs us $1.59 to provide a free meal for a hungry or homeless person. Our meals are the primary reason many people come to The Bowery Mission. Once they're here, we introduce them to the full services of our Mission and to the power of God to change lives.

We keep the cost of these meals as low as possible. That means that

most of our income is available to help provide the shelter, counseling, education and training that homeless people need. This is all part of a total rehabilitation process.

That's how your support of The Bowery Mission helps us provide meals and other essential care, and leads to restored, productive lives.

**How would you like to hear from us?**

We want to communicate with you in the most effective way possible. If you would like to change the amount of mail you receive from The Bowery Mission, visit us at www.bowery.org/mail for the Mail Preference Survey.

**I'd like to make my gift by credit card:**

[ ] VISA [ ] MasterCard [ ] DISCOVER [ ]

CARD NUMBER

EXP. DATE                                   AMOUNT $

CARDHOLDER'S NAME (please print)

CARDHOLDER'S SIGNATURE (required)

The Bowery Mission
227 Bowery
New York, NY
10002

**THE BOWERY MISSION**
**MURRAY HILL STATION**
**PO BOX 2000**
**NEW YORK NY 10157-2851**

---

## A few of the programs your donation will support!

**Outreach Program**
Our Outreach Van travels to parks and street corners in Manhattan and Brooklyn to serve individuals who may be wary or unaware of our services. The Outreach Van also provides critical bags of groceries for families forced to choose between food and rent.

**Discipleship Institute**
The Bowery Mission Discipleship Institute is a six-month residential recovery program for men who were once homeless. The Discipleship Institute incorporates one-on-one and group counseling, addiction recovery, career education and training at our on-site Career Center with on-the-job work experience.

**Transitional Center**
The Bowery Mission Transitional Center is a highly successful six- to nine-month residential recovery program, designed to transition formerly homeless, drug-addicted men into independent living.

**Women's Center**
The Bowery Mission Women's Center at Heartsease Home is a unique place of hope and healing — the only faith-based residential recovery program for homeless women in Manhattan. The Women's Center's structured program helps women build a hopeful future.

**Mont Lawn Camp**
Since 1894, Mont Lawn Camp has provided adventure for children from New York's toughest neighborhoods. More than 950 campers experience swimming, boating, rock climbing, camping and the close attention of our caring staff.

*"The Bowery Mission has served our city's most vulnerable citizens for more than a century and I congratulate you on your success. New York City has a tradition of providing for the neediest, and your organization stands as a terrific example of that compassion."*

Michael R. Bloomberg
Mayor, City of New York

*"I encourage everyone to support The Bowery Mission. Not only do they help people with food and shelter, they really make a positive difference in people's lives."*

Al Roker
NBC's The Today Show

The Bowery Mission

227 Bowery • New York, NY 10002 • 1-800-BOWERY-1 • www.bowery.org

---

## Longer lines a sign of the times ... but how long will they get this Thanksgiving?

NEW YORK — Since New York's economy hit the skids, it seems the lines outside The Bowery Mission have been getting longer and longer.

Lately, so many people have been coming for help that the Mission has had trouble keeping up.

"In my 16 years with the Mission, I can't remember it ever being this bad," noted Mission president Ed Morgan. "Every day, we're hearing from men, women and families who have never needed help before."

Last year during the Thanksgiving season, the Mission served more than 56,000 meals — and distributed 13,200 bags of groceries — to homeless and hungry people in our community. This year, those numbers could go even higher.

"When families come to us, they're desperate," says Morgan. "They've often exhausted all other avenues of help.

"We've promised them we'd help them. They're counting on us. I'm not going to let them down, not at Thanksgiving.

"How can Morgan be so sure — especially in such hard times?

"It's the generosity of this community," Morgan says. "1 in 139 years, our New York City community has been making it possible to provide food and other care to hurting people can get back on their feet."

"That's a big task, particularly when you consider that as many as one out of every 10

Hundreds of homeless men, women and hungry families will enjoy a Thanksgiving feast at The Bowery Mission this year. More than 24,000 meals will be served in November alone.

Americans goes to bed hungry each night.

If any place is up to the challenge, it's The Bowery Mission. The Mission provides emergency services throughout the year, but really rolls out the red carpet at Thanksgiving.

There are decorated holiday tables. Scores of helpful volunteers. Tons of good food. And because so much of it is donated, the Mission can provide a complete Thanksgiving dinner (including pumpkin pie for dessert) for just $1.59.

That's a big task, particularly when you consider that as many as one out of every 10

different reasons. Loss of a job. Home foreclosure. An illness. And breaking paychecks that don't keep up with rising prices.

Fortunately, the Mission is able to stretch every dollar it receives to help thousands with a variety of life-changing programs for men, women and children. Many are so grateful for the help they have received that they end up volunteering, so others might find the same hope they did.

This year, The Bowery Mission is asking for help again.

With your help,

*The Bowery Mission - A charity appeal with inserts and strong copy cosmetics*

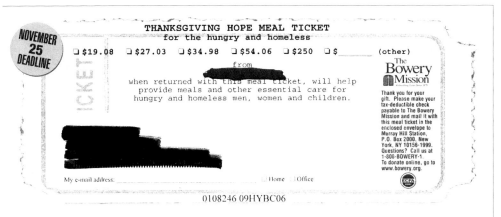

Dear ▮▮▮▮▮▮▮

    Thank you for joining with us to provide nutritious meals -- and hope -- for thousands of homeless and hungry men, women and children. And remember: A whole meal costs just $1.59!

    Please give what you can to feed the homeless in New York City. And don't forget to send your gift by November 25. A single meal is often the first step to a whole new life. Thank you!

*Ed Morgan*

*AHW IT LTD - A freelancer's letter of introduction: try ignoring this one!*

<<FirstName>><<LastName>>
<<JobTitle>>
<<Company>>
<<AddressLine1>>
<<AddressLine2>>
<<AddressLine3>> <<PostCode>>

Delivering Value

**AHW** IT LTD

T: 01633 663739
E: info@ahw-it.co.uk
W: www.ahw-it.co.uk
26 Cotswold Way, Newport NP19 9DL

## Did you know...?

96% of business owners in Wales
seriously think about

# throwing their computer out of the window

at least once a week!!

Dear [Name]

OK, I admit, I made that up (I had to grab your attention somehow)...BUT if there was a real survey on I.T. based hissy-fits, 96% is the kind of number I'd expect!

Why? Because after 25 years in the I.T. world, I still haven't met the MD who doesn't fume at their PC as soon as the Gremlins take charge.

**And let's be honest – I.T. Gremlins know exactly when to attack!**
They know when you're chasing a deadline, or when you're under-staffed. Then they get inside your system and slow it to a crawl...and in today's market, no-one can afford that kind of distraction.

**So - if you've cursed your PC this week, let me introduce myself...** *or turn over for a £185 freebie*
My name's Arend Westdorp, and as you've probably guessed, I'm a local I.T. Consultant. But (I can't stress this enough) I'm not one of the usual blind-you-with-techie-stuff types. I specialise in strictly-no-jargon, fitting-the-business kind of support.

I've talked to clients and other business owners, and I'd guess you want the same thing: a system that lets you and your staff get on with running the business...so it doesn't slow down, it doesn't lose data, and it's not built from cookie-cutter software that's scarcely fit for purpose.

**I know, this all sounds like an impossible dream!**
But I promise you, it's not. In 2010, there's no excuse for I.T. impacting on productivity. So if your team is still making do with networks, equipment and applications that just don't fit the bill, I guarantee I can turn things around.

✱ But you won't believe me yet...so my first job is on the house!

OVER....

*AHW IT LTD - A freelancer's letter of introduction: try ignoring this one!*

## Do any of these ~~problems~~ *I.T. HEADACHES* ring a bell?

*"My network's erratic!"..."My system's too slow!"..."My website is crashing the server!"..."My security settings are failing!"..."Nothing has worked since we added new software!"..."We're not using the full power of our applications!"*

Your efficiency could be compromised by any one of these gripes - or a few dozen others. The solution could lie in training, hardware, software, networks, databases...who knows?

**I.T. is a murky world - and no-one makes it through the labyrinth without a qualified guide!**

So, here's my first job for you. *(No charge, no obligation!)*
I'll give you a free consultation – normally £125 – to see what state your systems are in, understand the role of I.T. in your business and explore new ways of working that fit your business goals.

### ✳ It's free, as long as you call me by 14th May 2010 ✳

*BY THE WAY* I might not have worked in a business exactly like yours before...but since the mid 80s I've been tackling I.T. problems in all types of organisations, from the MOD to local SMEs...so there's not a single challenge I haven't seen before.

**So – can we talk?**
I know I can help you get the most from I.T. so your business runs at full pelt. But if you're still not sure, here's another shameless bribe for you!

---

If you call me <u>this month</u>, I'll also run a free health check on your machine – normally £60. In a couple of hours, we'll check for viruses, get rid of the deleted items clogging your memory banks and get it back to optimum speed.
*(And don't worry: I'll make a copy first so you can always roll back...)*

---

**My final word: FLEXIBILITY**
If you decide I'm a good fit for your business, you'll have (I think) the most flexible I.T. support package in South Wales!

✓ I only charge £30 an hour

✓ After the first hour, I bill in 15-minute strands *(so 61 minutes won't cost you 2 hours!)*

✓ There's no Gold-Silver-Bronze type of package...it's only what you need

*It has to be worth a chat! Let's talk...and you'll never get cross with your PC again – promise!*

Sincerely

*Arend Westdorp*

**Arend Westdorp**

**Call 01633 663739**
*or mail: Arend@AHW-IT.co.uk*

P.S. Remember, I'm offering a free consultation until 14th May...and if you call this month, I'll add a complete health-check for your PC. *Total value £185. You pay £0*

*Flamingo Dry Cleaning - A letter that uses humour to grab – and hold – attention*

**EXCLUSIVE DRY CLEANING OFFER**

# You're going to love this amazing deal... unless you're a Traffic Warden!

**FROM: Hemant Patel**
**Owner - Flamingo Dry Cleaning, Norbury**

Dear <<Salutation>> <<Surname>>

I'm expecting a picket line of Traffic Wardens outside my shop. Because I'm making an offer to residents right across the borough - and make no mistake, the wardens will be gunning for me!

Why?

Well, this is my shop here, on London Road in Norbury. And much to everyone's annoyance, it's smack bang on the red route.

So every warden knows, if a customer parks up for just a minute to drop off their dry cleaning, it's a chance to swoop in and slap on a ticket.

They call it "easy pickings".

The trouble is, my customers are going mad (well wouldn't you?)...so I've made up my mind to put things right. And this is how I'll do it:

Instead of asking customers to drop off and pick up, my team will do it all. From this month, you don't have to fight through the traffic and risk another parking ticket, because we'll collect your dry cleaning, then deliver it when it's ready.

All at a time to suit you - and for no extra charge. Yep, no wonder the Traffic Wardens are cursing me under their breath!

Now, as you're a local resident - and probably used to the traumas of parking by the shops - I figured you'd want to know all about this exclusive new service. So if you can spare me 2 minutes, I'll tell you how it works.

*Plus, I'll give you a shameless bribe...because I want you to give us a try.*

*Flamingo Dry Cleaning - A letter that uses humour to grab – and hold – attention*

Enclosed with this letter, you'll find a bag. Just fill it with anything that needs the professional touch: shirts, trousers, suits, coats, bed linen, blankets, table cloths, curtains...even leather and suede items. We take care of it all.

Once your bag is full, **let me know by calling 020 8765 8020 or texting your address + <u>PICKUP2</u> to 07983 321822**. One of my team will be there in a flash - and they'll agree a convenient time to bring it all back, freshly laundered.

By the way - there's no catch here.

There's no set-up fee, no long-term commitment and no hidden charges. Just call us any time you've got a full bag - worth £20 or more - and we'll get to work while you get on with other important stuff.

Impressed? I'm sure you will be...especially when you check out our prices:

---

**✻ Can you beat this?**

* Laundered Shirts (minimum 5):            £1.65 each
* Trousers:                                £4.45 each
* Suits:                                   £9.40 each
* Coats:                                   £10.30 each
* Ties:                                    £2.60 each
* Iron Only:                               £1.95 per lb
* Wash & Fold (6kg minimum):               £10.95 - then £1.50 per kg
* Bed Linen (duvet cover, bed sheet & 2 pillow cases):  £7.50
* Expert repairs, alterations and other items:  Ask for details
* Loyalty Scheme for frequent flyers

*I'll tell you more when you call...*

---

Now about that shameless bribe I promised. Actually you know what - here's two:

## <u>BRIBE #1</u>
## I'll Pay You £2 For Every Broken Button

Some Dry Cleaners (I'm naming no names) can be ham-fisted at times, and they'll send your favourite clothes back with buttons missing or broken. Not us. I'm going out on a limb and promising you £2 for every button that's lost or damaged.

Now, believe me I'm not saying this because I like giving money away! I'm a small business owner with big overheads, so I can't afford to dish out £2 here, there and everywhere.

No, I'm saying this because it's <u>your guarantee of quality</u>. You know I'll do anything to avoid paying you £2. So we'll be meticulous, checking every last detail before we send your dry cleaning back with that special crisp 'n' fresh feel.

*Flamingo Dry Cleaning - A letter that uses humour to grab – and hold – attention*

Ready for bribe number #2...? Here it is:

## BRIBE #2
## £10 Off Your First Order

Here's the thing: you don't know me yet, so I've got to prove to you that my business works to the highest standards. Sure, I can tell you that we're the longest established Dry Cleaners in South London...or that I've got 35 years experience in the industry...or that we've been voted 'Most Loved Dry Cleaners' in Croydon's Best of Borough Awards. But that's just reputation. You won't believe we're the real deal until you actually try us - so I'm making it easy by offering £10 off the first time we 'call and collect'.

### Ready? OK Let's Do This...

I really want you to give us a try. Remember, we do more than Dry Cleaning. We do Laundry, Ironing, Wash & Fold, Repairs & Alterations. Heck, we'll even recycle your hangers if you ask us nicely.

Basically, we're here to save you a whole lot of bother.

After all, life is busy. We all have to work long hours and there's not much family time, so why add to the hassle by sweating over laundry and ironing? <u>Send it here instead, and do something more fun with your time</u>. Go on - go to the pictures, ride a bike, go fishing, learn the trombone...do one of those things you keep putting off, because now the world's your oyster!!

### Place Your First Order Today
### Fill Your Bag and call 020 8765 8020
### Or text your address + PICKUP2 to 07983 321822

If you like us, you could go nuts and throw away your ironing board! But that's for later. Let's start with one bag, then see what you think.

Your £10 discount is valid until Thursday 31st July, so best do it now before 101 other things crop up...

I look forward to being of service - and showing you an easier way to keep your clothing, linen and curtains in mint condition.

Yours sincerely

*Hemant Patel*

**Hemant Patel**

P.S. All cleaning, repairs and alterations are carried out on our premises. Nothing is outsourced, because I keep a tight rein on quality. You'll see what I mean when you fill your bag and get in touch. Call 020 8765 8020. Or text your address + <u>PICKUP2</u> to 07983 321822.

*IMPORTANT: P.T.O. FOR VOUCHERS....*

*Flamingo Dry Cleaning - A letter that uses humour to grab – and hold – attention*

**CUT OUT AND PRESENT WHEN YOU PLACE YOUR FIRST ORDER**

## £10 Off

Your First Dry Cleaning Bill

DRY CLEANING BY FLAMINGO

EXPIRES: 31-07-14

## £2 Back

For Every Lost or

Damaged Button

DRY CLEANING BY FLAMINGO

VALID ANY TIME

## FREE

Replacement bag

for your next order

DRY CLEANING BY FLAMINGO

VALID ANY TIME

## FREE TRIAL

Collection & Delivery

of orders worth £20 or more

DRY CLEANING BY FLAMINGO

EXPIRES: 31-07-14

You can use all your vouchers together – so trial our free collect & deliver service by placing a £20 order...then use your £10 off voucher to halve the cost.

### Place Your First Order Today
**Fill Your Bag and call 020 8765 8020**
**Or text your address + PICKUP2 to 07983 321822**

### Dry Cleaning by Flamingo
**1449 London Road, Norbury, Surrey SW16 4AQ**

Most Loved Dry Cleaners - Croydon's Best of Borough Awards, 2009
Most Loved Dry Cleaners in the UK - Best Of UK Awards 2010

*Traffic Wardens can use this service too. You see, we bear no grudges!*

*Hamseys - A mattress sales piece, strong on copy and design*

# Crazy as it Sounds, You Can Take a Premium Mattress Home This Week...Sleep on it for 100 Nights...Then if it's not the Best Sleep of Your Life *JUST HAND IT BACK!*

**FROM THE DESK OF:** Simon Hunt
**Managing Director - Hamseys**

# HAMSEYS
━━━━ ESTABLISHED OVER 40 YEARS ━━━━

*FREE* **Fast Delivery**
*FREE* **Unwrap & Fitting**
*FREE* **Disposal of Your Old Mattress**
*FREE* **Mattress Protector**
*FREE* **Memory Foam Pillow**
**When you spend £500 or more**

**AND SAVE AT LEAST 50%**

Dear Mr Richards

Odd, isn't it?

We spend one third of our lives asleep - and yet most of us are making do with an old and saggy mattress!

It damages our sleep, and spoils our waking hours too.

It causes back trouble....stiffness....breathing problems.... restless nights. All leading to low energy and poor concentration.

In other words, we deny ourselves the rich sleep we deserve. The sleep we need, as much as food, to fuel our busy lives.

I think we can do better.

So if your mattress has seen better days...and you're left feeling the strain...I've got something important to share with you: a chance to sleep better than ever, by trialling *(yes, trialling)* a brand new deep sleeping mattress at home – and save a massive 50% off our usual store price.

*BUT this offer expires on* **Sunday 14th June.**
*So please give me 5 minutes now, to tell you more...*

*Feel like this in the morning? Don't!*

## OK....But why so urgent?

By the time your mattress is 5 years old, it's taken quite a battering. As we sleep, we can sweat out half a pint of bodily fluid, and every year we shed a whole pound of dead skin cells. That makes a haven for dust mites - a major cause of asthma.

What's more, all this wear and tear weakens the mattress from inside. Then countless nights of tossing and turning create an uneven surface....and so, as the mattress grows older, things

*Older mattresses attract more guests*

*Hamseys - A mattress sales piece, strong on copy and design*

keep getting worse.

# Scientists Agree: Change Your Mattress After 5 Years

In 2008, researchers at Oklahoma State University studied 59 people - a cross section of age, weight and gender - by observing their sleeping patterns over 56 nights.

Each participant spent half the nights on their own 5-year-old mattress. Then spent the remaining nights sound asleep on a brand new model.

### After sleeping on a new mattress....

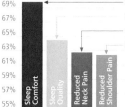

69.9% said *"Yes, I slept more comfortably"*

64.4% said *"Yes, It was better quality sleep"*

62.8% said *"Yes, it eased my back pain"*

62.4% said *"Yes, it eased my shoulder pain"*

*The results say it all: a new mattress makes a huge difference*

## The Question is: <u>Are You Ready?</u>

I know, science can say what it likes. But proof or no proof, changing your mattress is still a big decision - especially if you're from the Baby Boomer Generation, like me. Remember, we grew up in a world where nothing was disposable, where mattresses wouldn't be trashed until the springs were poking through!

That's how it was when a new mattress cost a whole month's wages. We learned to get by and work through all the ill effects. But today, a quality mattress is more affordable than ever - so you don't have to soldier on.

**Grab a pen and see if the time is right:**

# 7 Sure Signs That Your Mattress is on its Way Out

I agree ✓

**1** "I can feel ridges, lumps or springs prodding me in bed" ☐

**2** "When I move in bed, I hear creaks and crunches inside the mattress" ☐

**3** "There's a dip in the mattress - so we're both rolling into the centre!" ☐

**4** "I find it hard to sleep, because I'm not breathing easily" ☐

**5** "I wake up with neck or back pain at least 2 mornings a week" ☐

**6** "I'm tired at the start of the day....I need more zest, more energy" ☐

**7** "My mattress looks old and shabby. I'd die of shock if the neighbours saw it!" ☐

*Every tick says it's time for change. So....what are your options?*

*Hamseys - A mattress sales piece, strong on copy and design*

# Pocket Sprung or Memory Foam...or the best of both?

Mattresses have come a long way since the days of the coiled spring. Today, the most popular systems - **Pocket Sprung** and **Memory Foam** - offer much more support and comfort for a deep, relaxing sleep.

**Pocket Sprung** is ultra-supportive. Each spring sits inside its own fabric pocket, moving on its own - not buckling or bending to the shape of the springs around it.

That means partners won't roll-together (remember the hippo and duck?)....and with a built-in shock absorber, there's less pressure on the back, neck and shoulder.

What's more, our best models are easy to care for: rotate now and then, but don't turn! And with covering to protect against dust mites, they're kind on allergies too.

**Backcare Extreme by Sleepeezee**
1000 springs for gentle lumber support.
**SAVE OVER £300**

**The Royal (with Royal pedigree!)**
William & Kate's 4500 spring mattress.
*Feel the luxury!*
**SAVE OVER £1100**

**Memory Plus**
Just sink into the foam and drift away
**SAVE OVER £240**

**Memory Foam** is all about comfort. It adapts to the shape of your body, then springs back to its original form - so you can sink into a long deep sleep and change position, undisturbed.

Back pain sufferers love it, because it keeps the spine naturally aligned. But it's not just for pain relief - it's a great release from tension, that's popular with all kinds of people who lead stressful lives.

*Torn between choices?*
*There's a third way...*

# Super Cool: a mattress with balanced support that moulds to the shape of your body....and keeps you cool at night

We hate to boast - but **Super Cool** might be the world's smartest mattress. A hybrid of memory foam and pocket springs, that hugs you all night long.

The springs below support you, the foam above envelops you.... and thanks to a unique cooling gel that draws heat from the foam, you can sleep the whole night through without throwing off the duvet!

**Super Cool**
The smartest mattress ever?
Only you can decide....
**SAVE OVER £500**

**Interested?**
**OK - So let's make this easy...**

*Hurry! Offer ends Sunday 14th June*

*Hamseys - A mattress sales piece, strong on copy and design*

# HALF PRICE MATTRESS SALE!

## Save AT LEAST 50% on a Brand New Mattress

As you're a valued customer, I'm inviting you to order a new mattress today - or any time this month - and we'll take at least 50% off the RRP.

And it's your choice: take The Royal, Memory Plus, Backcare Extreme...even The Super Cool...or any other mattress you see here in our Beckenham store.

You'll find dozens of designs here, to fit any size bed (even non-standards). Plus, you can choose your tension - mid or firm - for **ULTRA or EXTRA** Support.

**It's like having your own mattress custom-made... without the ridiculous price tag!**

| MEMORY PLUS | WAS | NOW | SAVE |
|---|---|---|---|
| Single | £240.00 | £99.95 | £140.05 |
| Double | £360.00 | £119.95 | £240.05 |
| Kingsize | £400.00 | £149.95 | £250.05 |
| SLEEPEEZEE BACKCARE | WAS | NOW | SAVE |
| Single | £450.00 | £225.00 | £225.00 |
| Double | £600.00 | £299.95 | £300.05 |
| Kingsize | £700.00 | £349.95 | £350.05 |
| DREAMFLEX SUPERCOOL | WAS | NOW | SAVE |
| Single | £800.00 | £399.95 | £400.05 |
| Double | £1,000.00 | £499.95 | £500.05 |
| Kingsize | £1,200.00 | £599.95 | £600.05 |
| Super Kingsize | £1,400.00 | £699.95 | £700.05 |
| THE ROYAL MATTRESS | WAS | NOW | SAVE |
| Single | £1,800.00 | £849.95 | £950.05 |
| Double | £2,100.00 | £999.95 | £1,100.05 |
| Kingsize | £2,200.00 | £1,099.95 | £1,100.05 |
| Super Kingsize | £3,500.00 | £1,499.95 | £2,000.05 |

*Sample prices only - ask about other sizes and models*

*Wake up ready to face the world!*

## EXCLUSIVE: Trial Your New Mattress at Home for 100 Nights

I want you to give your new mattress a thorough road test! So sleep on it for 100 nights. **That's over 3 months, or 800 hours of testing.** Then you can decide:

**Love it? Great - you're sleeping better. Everyone's happy!**

Can't get used to it? No problem. Trade it back for a different model, or walk away and **we'll refund your investment 100%.** *(YES, REALLY!)*

**100% SATISFACTION GUARANTEED**

*Just bring this voucher into the store BEFORE 4pm on Sunday 14th June*

Our team of mattress experts, with over 50 years combined experience, is here to help you get the perfect night's sleep.

We can't nip round every night and sing lullabies... we can't bring you steaming hot cocoa...but we can give you a gentle, supportive mattress for the most restful sleep of your life.

I'm looking forward to seeing you here in Beckenham - soon.

*Simon Hunt*

**Simon Hunt - Managing Director**

P.S. Please remember, this offer is for valued customers only - so be sure to bring the voucher with you!

*P.P.S. Order by midday for FREE Same Day Delivery...and sleep on your brand new mattress TONIGHT*

### HAMSEYS
**VALUED CUSTOMER OFFER**
*AT LEAST 50% OFF Any Mattress - PLUS:*
- FREE Fast Delivery, Unwrap & Fitting
- FREE Disposal of Your Old Mattress
- FREE Mattress Protector
- FREE Pillow Set
- EXCLUSIVE 100 Night Trial: trade in or return your mattress in the next 100 days

Minimum £500 spend.
Subject to availability.
Expires Sunday 14th June 2015

# HAMSEYS
ESTABLISHED OVER 40 YEARS

**421 CROYDON ROAD, BECKENHAM, KENT BR3 3PP**

Monday to Saturday: **9am - 6pm** | Sunday: **11am - 5pm** Enquiries: **020 8658 2242** | beckenham@hamseys.co.uk

*Gary Halbert's Coat-of-Arms Letter - A compelling single pager from a copywriting legend*

5687 Ira Road
Bath, Ohio   44210

Phone: 1-216-666-9356

Dear Mr. Macdonald,

Did you know that your family name was recorded with a coat-of-arms in ancient heraldic archives more than seven centuries ago?

My husband and I discovered this while doing some research for some friends of ours who have the same last name as you do. We've had an artist recreate the coat-of-arms exactly as described in the ancient records. This drawing, along with other information about the name, has been printed up into an attractive one-page report.

The bottom half of the report tells the story of the very old and distinguished family name of Macdonald. It tells what the name means, its origin, the original family motto, its place in history and about famous people who share it. The top half has a large, beautiful reproduction of an artist's drawing of the earliest known coat-of-arms for the name of Macdonald. This entire report is documented, authentic and printed on parchment-like paper suitable for framing.

The report so delighted our friends that we have had a few extra copies made in order to share this information with other people of the same name.

Framed, these reports make distinctive wall decorations and they are great gifts for relatives. It should be remembered that we have not traced anyone's individual family tree but have researched back through several centuries to find out about the <u>earliest</u> people named Macdonald.

All we are asking for them is enough to cover the added expenses of having the extra copies printed and mailed. (See below.) If you are interested, please let us know right away as our supply is pretty slim. Just verify that we have your correct name and address and send the correct amount in cash or check for the number of reports you want. We'll send them promptly by return mail.

Sincerely,

*Nancy L. Halbert*

P.S. If you are ordering only one report, send two dollars ($2.00). Additional reports ordered at the same time and sent to the same address are one dollar each. Please make checks payable to me, Nancy L. Halbert.

*General Utilities - A simple home heating offer, mailed in a paper bag*

*Full Service Oil Delivery - Home of Long Island's Cap Price*
*Your Home Heating Solution Partner*

# General Utilities

100 Fairchild Avenue, Plainview, NY 11803
800.290.9202 - www.generalutilities.com

Not sure who to trust with your home heating this winter? Too many oil companies all shouting at you?

Well, let me give you a reason... in fact 100 reasons ... to go with General. How about $100 off your first delivery? Call our sales promotion number, 800.290.9202, sign up with General and you'll receive the discount immediately!

Of course you get far more than $100 in savings, like guaranteed below market pricing for the life of your contract....guaranteed 24 x 7 x 365 service (the Island's best... a variety of program and payment options just right for your budget....a "Cap Price" program that limits the price of what you'll pay no matter how high the global oil market rises this winter but drops if the market does... the peace of mind that we'll be there for you all day/every day.

Give us a call. Enjoy a hundred bucks off your first delivery and a hundred reasons why General should be your oil company.

Warm Regards,

Joe DeFelice, General Manager
joseph@generalutilities.com

---

**GENERAL UTILITIES**
New Customer Promotion - Valid Through **2010**
Call Today: **800.290.9202**

# $100
# General Bucks Certificate

**Applicable Towards the First Delivery on a One Year Oil Contract with General Utilities**
**Call Today 800.290.9202 and Immediately Enjoy Savings on Your Home Heating**

Nassau License H24034100 - Suffolk License 2124RP3256RE

*General Utilities - A simple home heating offer, mailed in a paper bag*

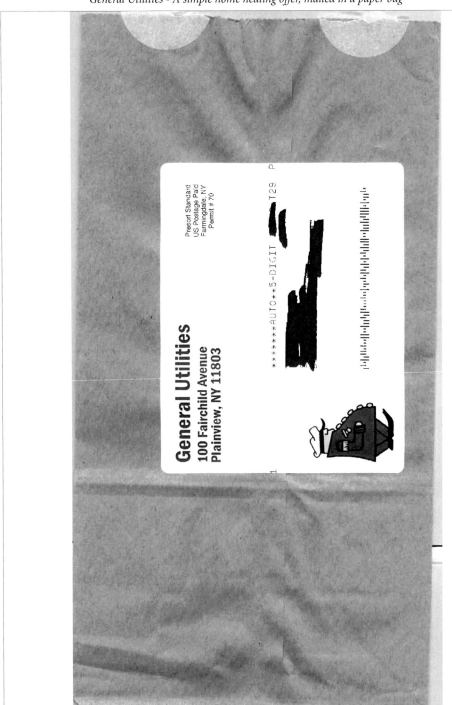

*General Utilities - A simple home heating offer, mailed in a paper bag*

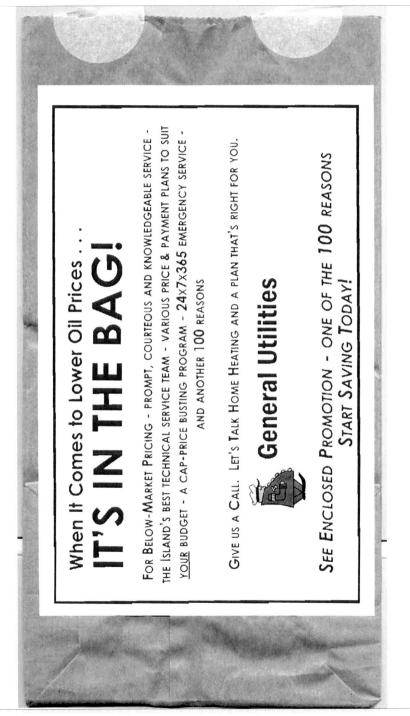

*FC&A Medical - Long copy works! This letter takes 8 pages to sell a book*

**Frank K. Wood**
**FC&A Medical Publishing**
**103 Clover Green**
**Peachtree City, GA 30269**

From Frank K. Wood

Dear Customer,

Do you know what the _number_ _one_ _cause_ _of_ _death_ for both men and women has been every year for the last 99 years? It's not cancer ... and it's not accidents. It's heart disease.

According to the Centers For Disease Control And Prevention, heart disease is responsible for the death or hospitalization of 21 Million unsuspecting people like YOU and ME every year.

I was especially shocked to hear this because I know for a fact that **it's easy to safely and naturally prevent or relieve heart disease**! For example:

* _One_ _meal-time_ _BEVERAGE_ _will_ _SLASH_ _your_ _risk_ _of_ _HEART_ _DISEASE_ _by_ _50%_ -- _but_ _you_ _must_ _drink_ _the_ _right_ _amount_ _every_ _day_.

* COFFEE ALERT! If you, like millions, enjoy a good cup of joe, you need to know that by switching your brand of coffee you can lower your cholesterol by 10%.

* _This_ _household_ _item_ _is_ _a_ _powerful_ _CLOT-BUSTER_ _that_ _if_ _taken_ _in_ _the_ _right_ _amount_ _at_ _the_ _onset_ _of_ _a_ _heart_ _attack_ _can_ _DRAMATICALLY_ _INCREASE_ _your_ _chance_ _of_ _SURVIVAL_.

Friend, there are literally hundreds more of these perfectly natural healthy-heart CURES that _work_ _better_ _than_ _any_ _risky_ _surgery_ and cost ONLY PENNIES a day. There are hundreds of safe, natural REMEDIES you can take WITHOUT PRE-SCRIPTION that _make_ _dangerous_ _drugs_ _obsolete_.

And if you're already taking prescriptions for your heart, cholesterol or blood pressure, I've uncovered little-known research you need to know to _ensure_ _your_ _medicines_ _work_ _best_ ... _and_ _don't_ _end_ _up_ _harming_ _you_.

I've compiled over 1,323 of these little-known healthy-heart secrets in a brand new book I just finished called **Healthy Heart Handbook**.

_I believe these healthy-heart secrets are so important that I want to send this brand new book to you absolutely free for 30 days!_

**You will feel better, have more energy and live longer!**

Within minutes of cracking open this invaluable, leading-edge guide for your heart, you'll see that _you_ _don't_ _have_ _to_ _be_ _a_ _victim_ _of_ _heart_ _disease_. You don't have to go through painful surgery or take dangerous drugs for the rest of your life. And here's a nice surprise ...

(go to page 2)

*FC&A Medical - Long copy works! This letter takes 8 pages to sell a book*

-- page 2 --

You DON'T have to give up the things you love -- like meat and desserts and taking it easy -- just to try and stay healthy.

Unfortunately, you doctor will NEVER share these life-saving healthy heart secrets with you. Why? Partly because he's just not taught to think about them. And partly because the medical establishment won't let him. The hospitals and drug companies can't make any money off of anything "natural".

That's why I've made it my business for the past 25 years to keep up on all the latest natural miracle healers. This is vital information that often takes years to reach the general public. These cures simply can't wait. These are all-natural remedies for your heart that don't require a doctor ... or a prescription ... or a hospital. Now you'll find them all, like these, as soon as you open your new copy of the **Healthy Heart Handbook**:

* Eat pasta, cheese ... even red meat! Discover the food pyramid from the mediterranean country where people live longer and suffer fewer disease than anywhere on earth! Page 164.

* A handful of nuts may be the easiest way of all to protect your heart. Page 286 tells which ones are best for you.

* Want to cut your risk of heart attack by a whopping 30%? Just add 10 grams a day to your diet of any of the 10 tasty foods listed on page 113.

* ATTENTION CHOCOLATE LOVERS! You already know how good chocolate tastes ... research now proves that chocolate can be good for your heart. Get all the exciting details on page 123.

* The trace enzyme CoQ10 fights heart disease 10 important ways. Page 135 gives the details and how to make sure you're getting enough.

* Evidence shows that the 5 herbs mentioned on page 239 can improve your heart health without having to rely on dangerous drugs or surgery.

* Grab your toothbrush and reduce heart disease by up to 25% The amazing facts behind this unlikely discovery on page 229 of the **Healthy Heart Handbook**.

* Surprising role of pizza in slashing your heart risk 50%. Page 339 gives you all the information you need.

**Rumors and myths uncovered! Learn the life-saving truth about heart attack, high blood pressure and cholesterol, food and medicine.**

* STOP WORRYING ... the totally harmless heart "attack" that scares most people half to death. Revealed on page 8.

* 6 signs of heart attack that must NEVER be ignored ... and the simple, little-known step that dramatically increase your chances of survival. This life-saving secret alone makes this book indispensible. Page 11.

* 7 simple steps to naturally lowering blood pressure. Page 36.

* Lower your cholesterol 30%. You won't believe how easy. Page 58.

* Whole? Half? Baby? Daily? Weekly? Don't be confused by rumors and

(go to page 3)

*FC&A Medical - Long copy works! This letter takes 8 pages to sell a book*

-- page 3 --

misinformation. *Get the life-saving truth about the the exact dose of aspirin that can prevent heart attack and save your life.* It's all explained on page 70.

* Mom was right! New study shows drinking your milk is REALLY good for you -- slashing your risk of stroke in half! But only the kind and amount shown on page 93 will work. Check it out.

* Fiber is good ... But are you getting the right kind? It makes all the difference in the world. Explained on page 115.

* Take the caffeine quiz on page 138. The answers may surprise you ... and change your life.

* You'll be surprised how much fat is in "fat-free" food. Page 157 of the **Healthy Heart Handbook** takes the mystery out of food label double-talk for you.

* INCREDIBLE! Normal blood pressure in 2 weeks ... without medication. Page 161.

* The truth about estrogen therapy and menopause -- 6 reasons your heart will benefit. Fully explained on page 182.

* Headache ... or heart attack? Researchers at a prestigious medical center in New York have discovered that some headache pain -- NOT chest pain -- indicates an oncoming heart attack. *Find out how to tell the difference on page 196.* This can save your life.

* Which fruit contains the most vitamin C? Nope, it's not oranges. *The fruit on page 353 gives you the most vitamin C and helps reduce your risk of heart disease by up to 50%.*

* Fishy chicken. By adding the natural grain on page 217 to their diets, farmers are breeding a chicken that gives you all the benefits of fish oil and has way less cholesterol.

* Save time and money on doctor visits by 87%! This is proven by insurance studies. And you don't even have to leave your chair. Page 301.

* Shop for color and cut your risk of heart attack and stroke in half. *Researchers prove the more colorful the fruits and vegetables you eat the more they're packed with the heart-friendly nutrient on page 345.*

* Researchers studied two groups of people who already had heart disease. After 6 months, one group had 77% fewer heart attacks. The only difference? See page 358.

**Finally get the whole story.**
**Life-saving facts about cholesterol that you need to know!**

* New cholesterol DANGER! There's a newly discovered cholesterol that DOUBLES your risk of having a heart attack, but *doesn't respond to conventional cholesterol treatments.* Here's what you should do. See page 23 right away.

* Do-It-Yourself cholesterol test for under $20! Now available. Page 23 has the details.

(go to page 4)

*FC&A Medical - Long copy works! This letter takes 8 pages to sell a book*

-- page 4 --

* BEWARE taking too much of the vitamin on page 25! Many people take it
  to help reduce cholesterol by up to 50%. But *overuse can cause serious
  liver damage.* See page 25.

* FDA bans Chinese secret that lowers cholesterol by 18% A Federal judge
  overruled the ban ... for now. See page 29 to find out how to get this
  powerful natural healer.

* Can this funny little vegetable on page 68 really improve your cholesterol as effectively as dangerous prescription drugs? Researchers say
  it's true. Try it yourself to get immediate benefit.

* MORE DANGEROUS THAN CHOLESTEROL! Homocysteine is a natural by-product
  of your metabolism that is *more closely linked to heart disease than
  anything else* -- even cholesterol. Fortunately, it's much easier to
  control than cholesterol. Page 78 tells you how.

* New help for reducing cholesterol is as close as your next piece of
  toast. Page 90 explains the secret.

* Fats are bad ... right? Not necessarily. Page 105 straightens it all
  out and shows you how to get the right amount of the one fat that will
  actually help slash bad cholesterol and increase the good.

* *There is a compound* of red yeast rice which has been used for thousands
  of years in Chinese cooking ... and it will lower your dangerous cholesterol by 18%. Page 28.

* If you've stayed away from shrimp and other shellfish for fear of their
  higher cholesterol content, the research explained on page 210 will
  have you reaching for the cocktail sauce in no time.

* Zap cholesterol with the tasty 1-2 punch on page 209.

* Try these cholesterol-busters you grow right in your garden. They can
  slash your cholesterol by 20% or more! Page 255.

**Forget about bland and restrictive "diets"! Just follow these simple food rec-
ommendations to beat heart disease and add years to your life!**

* 8 out of 10 people who follow this tasty, nutritious food plan have
  *blood vessels that look as clean and clear as if there never was any
  heart disease.* This could be a life-saver for you! Page 166.

* SWEET POISON! This popular candy can raise your blood pressure and
  strain your heart! Details on page 42.

* The truth about "Yo-Yo" dieting. This time it's good news for you!
  Other dieting myths squashed on page 364.

* Life-saving Southern hospitality! Southern cooking is notorious for
  being fatty, greasy and generally heart-unhealthy. *But this southern
  favorite has been found to dramatically lower "bad" cholesterol and
  raise the "good".* Find out what it is and how to get this tasty food
  on page 22.

* Beware the grapefruit effect! Ordinarily grapefruit juice is a nutritious and delicious snack. But researchers now know that taken with

(go to page 5)

*FC&A Medical - Long copy works! This letter takes 8 pages to sell a book*

-- page 5 --

some blood pressure medication, *grapefruit juice may lead to toxic lev-els of the medicine in your blood.* Find out what other drugs may be affected by grapefruit juice on page 41.

*   <u>Is</u> <u>wine</u> <u>heart-smart</u> <u>or</u> <u>not</u>? You've heard both sides of the argument. Find out what the experts say is best for your health on page 43.

*   <u>An</u> <u>apple</u> <u>a</u> <u>day</u>? Get the truth about adding years to your life with this sweet, crunchy snack. Page 58

*   <u>Butter</u> <u>or</u> <u>margarine</u>? The truth may surprise you. Page 87.

*   <u>Unscramble</u> <u>the</u> <u>confusion</u> over eggs and good health. Page 173.

*   <u>Lactose</u> <u>intolerant</u>? See page 95 for a dairy alternative you and your heart will love.

*   <u>Put</u> <u>elasticity</u> <u>and</u> <u>life</u> <u>back</u> into your hardened arteries with the deli-cious food named on page 219. (*That it also slashes your cholesterol by 20% is a side-benefit!*)

*   <u>Want</u> <u>to</u> <u>live</u> <u>longer</u>? The potent herb on page 232 works 5 ways to increase your life.

*   <u>Cut</u> <u>the</u> <u>fat</u> ... carefully. Don't struggle with cutting fat. *In fact, if you go too low, you'll actually do more harm than good.* Get the straight story on page 262 of the **Healthy Heart Handbook**.

*   <u>NO</u> <u>MORE</u> <u>BLAND</u> <u>FOOD</u>! Before you cut salt out of your diet take the easy test on page 311 to gauge your salt sensitivity. Many people can go back to using as much as they want with *no increase in blood pressure.*

*   <u>Tea</u> <u>time</u>. Researchers have found that ordinary tea is packed with heart-friendly flavanoids. See page 335 for full details.

*   <u>Want</u> <u>to</u> <u>lose</u> <u>some</u> <u>weight</u>? The 6 sure-fire tips on page 370 are *proven to work* even when nothing else has.

<u>Your</u> <u>life</u> <u>IS</u> <u>in</u> <u>your</u> <u>hands.</u> <u>Things</u> <u>you</u> <u>can</u> <u>do</u> <u>right</u> <u>now</u> <u>to</u> <u>beat</u> <u>heart</u> <u>disease</u> <u>and</u> <u>live</u> <u>a</u> <u>longer,</u> <u>happier</u> <u>life.</u>

*   <u>EXERCISE</u> <u>WARNING</u>! Whatever you do, do NOT exercise after drinking this common beverage on page 195 ... *especially if you have high blood pres-sure.* The results could be disastrous.

*   <u>Researchers</u> <u>have</u> <u>discovered</u> <u>a</u> <u>new</u> <u>personality</u> <u>identifier</u> that QUADRU-PLES the likelihood of death from heart disease for those who match. *You need to see page 53 to find out where you stand* ... and to get a simple, 10-step program to prolong your life.

*   <u>Over</u> <u>half</u> of the men who die suddenly from heart disease have this in common. How about you? See page 7.

*   <u>Why</u> <u>you</u> <u>should</u> <u>check</u> <u>with</u> <u>your</u> <u>weatherman</u> to prevent an emergency visit with your doctor. Answers on page 14.

*   <u>Forget</u> <u>anything</u> <u>you've</u> <u>heard</u> ... *there is ONLY one way to defend against dying from high blood pressure!* For the sake of your entire family, see page 33 NOW!

(go to page 6)

DIRECT MAIL 101                                          APPENDIX: SUCCESSFUL SALES LETTERS

*FC&A Medical - Long copy works! This letter takes 8 pages to sell a book*

-- page 6 --

* Like to relax in a steamy tub?  This favorite stress-buster can actually skyrocket your blood pressure.  *But don't give up your tub.*  Just
  check page 42 for the symptoms you should watch.

* 3 types of people proven to benefit from moderate drinking.  Page 46.

* Your personality can dramatically increase your risk of heart attack.
  Find out how at risk you are ... and easy ways to change ... on page 51
  of the **Healthy Heart Handbook**.

* Beat stress and get a good internal workout while sitting on your sofa.
  Amazing but true.  See page 55.

* For years doctors told us to stay away from coffee because it causes
  heart disease.  Now a study of 85,000 people says drink all you want
  ... but be careful of this on page 140.

* 13 ways to control stress.  You'll live longer and happier with these
  proven tips on page 251.

* 85% of those with high blood pressure became completely free of their
  medicine when they followed the simple advice on page 261.

* 20 effortless ways to cut fat that you'll never even miss.  Page 265.

**Say "NO" to dangerous surgery and harmful drugs.**
**Here's what you must know.**

* Which is more deadly for you -- cholesterol or your cholesterol-lower-
  ing prescription?  Find out on the chart on page 26.

* KILLER SURGERY?  Before you agree to any type of heart surgery -- even
  the supposedly "less-invasive" kind -- *you better know the results of
  this major medical study* on Page 17.

* Hospital report cards ... would you rather trust your life to a "top
  10" hospital or one that "flunked out"?  See where yours ranks on Page
  17.

* Invisible killer ... researchers have now discovered why many people
  with no known risk factors end up becoming heart vitamins.  *This means
  you may soon be able to completely prevent heart disease* with a common
  pill now on the market.  See page 10.

* Simple headache?  Before you reach for that ibuprofen, acetaminophen or
  aspirin, better check pages 13 and 14.  *Depending on your prescription
  medicine, these innocent painkillers could end up killing you!*

* Before you go under the knife ... 7 simple steps guaranteed to prevent
  unnecessary surgery and ensure you make it through any operation with
  flying colors.  Page 15 - 17.

* Heart deaths slashed 28%!  But only one of the many types of cholesterol drugs can make this claim.  *If it's not the one you're on, better
  get to your doctor fast!*  Check out page 24.

* Reduce your chance of dying from heart disease by 500%  Just ask your
  doctor to take your blood pressure again -- around your ankle.

(go to page 7)

*FC&A Medical - Long copy works! This letter takes 8 pages to sell a book*

-- page 7 --

Discover the life-saving formula on page 35.

* "Use with great caution, if at all ..." This is now the frightening recommendation of the National Heart, Lung and Blood Institute regarding a popular prescription blood pressure medicine. Find out if it's yours ... and what to do about it ... on page 37.

* Death in your medicine cabinet. If you take calcium channel blockers, you need to call your doctor NOW. You're may be at higher risk for cancer and an increase in heart attacks and death. Discover safer alternatives on page 37 of the *Healthy Heart Handbook*.

* LOOK OUT! Aspirin is the new "miracle drug" proven to save lives. But if you have any of the eight conditions listed on page 71, it can make your health problems worse.

* If your doctor has told you your arteries are clogged, the 10,000-year-old remedy on page 215 will help clean them out like a natural roto-rooter.

* Doctors are quick to recommend costly prescriptions. But not many know that the natural, inexpensive mineral on page 275 can heal your heart 6 vital ways ... with no side effects!

**Over 25 years and thousands of satisfied customers ensure the
*Healthy Heart Handbook* will change your life.**

Since I first began publishing little-known medical secrets over 25 years ago, my files have been bursting with letter after letter like those below of customers who testify that information in my various books changed their lives. I know the *Healthy Heart Handbook* will be no exception. (Note: In some cases, names, places and other details have been changed to ensure the privacy of our customers. Individual results vary.)

*"I have many, many medical books about natural healing and home remedies. This book had paid for itself by page #27."* Tana Grace, Gardena, CA

*"For many years my best friend Barbara has been suffering with [a serious illness]. I told Barbara to ...[from your book] And low and behold what a terrific response! The relief of all that pain and misery has vanished. What an amazing result -- thanks to your wonderful book."* Dorothy Rolick, Rochester, NY

*"... you saved the day! I have been coughing for 2 1/2 years not knowing what's going on with me. I have been to 5 doctors and even had sinus x-rays done. So, by reading your book I found out I was allergic to my own blood pressure medicine. Thanks so very much for having this article in your book."* Marilyn Myers, Huntington, IN

*"I find it very informative and easy to read and understand. In the past month my blood pressure has lowered from 180/110 to 150/90 and still on a downward trend, due mainly to information in that book."* John Ciccarelli, Mississauga, Ontario.

**Do not send any money!
I want you to use this life-saving book absolutely free for 30 days!**

(go to page 8)

*FC&A Medical - Long copy works! This letter takes 8 pages to sell a book*

-- page 8 --

I just can't stand to see one more person ... especially you ... suffer or even die unnecessarily of heart disease. That's why, with your permission, I will send you the **Healthy Heart Handbook** absolutely free of cost or obligation for 30 days.

PLEASE read it. Absorb it. Enjoy it. And most of all apply its life-saving tips to yourself and all those you love. Only then, after you've proven to yourself how valuable this book is, will I ask you to pay just 4 easy payments of only $6.99. And that's not all ...

<u>I guarantee you will be satisfied forever ...
with my "No-Time-Limit" money-back guarantee.</u>

You see, my **Healthy Heart Handbook** is an invaluable guide that will change your life forever ... not just 30 days. So if you <u>ever</u> become dissatisfied with it, I'll expect you to return it for a full refund. That's the way I've done business for over 25 years. You can't lose!

All you have to do to receive your **Healthy Heart Handbook** free for 30 days ... and then, guaranteed for life ... is return the order card in the enclosed postage paid envelope within 10 days. I promise I'll rush your book right out.

Sincerely,

*Frank K Wood*

Frank K. Wood

P.S. FREE BONUS GIFTS! Get 2 free "his & hers" credit card size calculators as a free bonus just for allowing me to send you my Healthy Heart Handbook without cost or obligation for 30 days. Please keep these "thank you" gifts even if you return the book. But my supplies are limited. To guarantee you get this bonus gift, please return the reply card within the next 10 days. Thank you.

*FC&A Medical - Long copy works! This letter takes 8 pages to sell a book*

```
#10 window envelope
```

FC&A MEDICAL PUBLISHING
**HEALTHY HEART HANDBOOK**
103 CLOVER GREEN
PEACHTREE CITY, GA 30269

PRESORTED STANDARD
U.S. POSTAGE PAID
FC&A

**Please! Use These 1,323 Safe, Natural Secrets To CLEAN OUT YOUR ARTERIES, LOWER YOUR BLOOD PRESSURE AND CHOLESTEROL! Save Yourself From The #1 Cause Of Death In America ... Without Dangerous Drugs Or Surgery!**

Dear Sample A Sample,
Before you finish this message,
Heart Disease will claim another victim.
See inside for how you can be spared,
feel better and live longer!

\*\*\*\*\*\*\*\*\*\*\*\*\*\*\*\*\*\*\*\*\*\*\*\*\*\*\*\*\*AUTO\*\*\*\*\*\*\*\*\*\*\*\*\*\*
Code
Sample A. Sample
1234 Main St.
Anytown, ST 12345

---

**SWEET POISON!** ... This popular candy can raise your blood pressure and strain your heart!

pic of candy

pic of veggies

**CHOLESTEROL-BUSTERS FROM YOUR OWN GARDEN!**
Safely slash cholesterol by 20%

**HOW THIS FUNNY LITTLE VEGETABLE SAFELY LOW-ERS YOUR CHOLESTEROL**
as effectively as dangerous pre-scriptions.

pic of artichoke

**THE TRUTH ABOUT COFFEE AND YOUR HEART!**
It can actually be good for you!

pic of cup of coffee

*Men's Fitness - A subscription letter with a distinctive layout and tone*

## Men's Fitness

# Do you have 5 hours for the gym today? Ha!

**Dear Fellow Realist:**

One magazine understands that fitness, while critical to our success, is a means. Not an end.

*Men's Fitness...*

- Stuff YOU can learn fast: high-impact abs in 30 days... a 15-minute upper torso routine... bigger arms in half the time

- Stuff YOU can make happen: improving your immunity with break-through herbal supplements... instant stress busting strategies... tricking your muscles into growing

- Stuff that DOESN'T SUCK: staying gut free forever... an exercise plan better than Viagra... high-octane eating for improved performance in the bedroom and the boardroom... and turning back the aging clock

Simply put: **We're fitness for the 21st century man.**

And you can have it now, FREE. Drop the enclosed card in the mail. I'll send you the next issue of the fastest-paced magazine ever created for guys like you. With no strings. If it's not for you, pay nothing.

### Fitness for the long haul?

*Men's Fitness* is about reality -- about achieving personal mastery with minimum output... for a lifetime.

I'm not talking fantasyland here.

We keep you in the groove about today's fitness. Today's adventure travel. Today's gear. Today's women. And today's sophisticated man. With no watered down maybes. No leaps of faith.

AND no holds barred.

Month after month you can thumb through a far-reaching life authority and see things you haven't seen before.

*Men's Fitness* is for movement forward, for growth. Without compromise, confusion, or true confessions.

Smart guy stuff. Stuff that DOESN'T SUCK.

Expect proof? Of course! Request your trial copy. I'll send you the next issue FREE. Then you'll see.

Best regards,

*Joe Weider*

Joe Weider
Publisher

**P.S. BONUS:** After you look over your free review copy and decide to subscribe, I'll send you our exclusive yearlong training guide, **The Men's Fitness Ultimate Program...** also **FREE**.

You get 40 pages packed with realistic tips on weights, cardio workouts and power foods. Mail the card now so together we can get on with the business of high-performance living.

*Hidden Hearing - A strong visual letter with the added punch of a coupon*

## HIDDEN HEARING
WE LISTEN, YOU HEAR

# A NEW YEAR
# A NEW START

### TAKE A NEW HEARING TEST
### AND HEAR BETTER IN 2016

**Book Your Next Hearing Test Today**

**& WIN £250 M&S VOUCHERS***

Dr. Hilary Jones
GP and TV Doctor

Dear Mr/s Sample

Remember New Year's Eve? The chiming of Big Ben, the sounds of laughter and celebration, and the joyful singing of Auld Lang Syne?

Hopefully, you enjoyed the first sounds that brought in the New Year.

Sadly though, for anyone who suffers with hearing loss, happy occasions like this can be quite an ordeal. So many people find, they feel isolated even though they're surrounded by their family and friends. The loud music and background chatter make hearing a constant struggle...so often, they'll end up sat alone in a corner, or pretending to join in.

**If you've had this experience recently, Hidden Hearing can help - and make sure you don't miss out at another get-together.**

I'm saying this because, contrary to myth, most types of hearing loss can be treated. In the last few years, hearing technology has come on leaps and bounds. So you can forget those ancient hearing aids that weighed a ton and made whistling noises! Modern devices are tiny and lightweight, and most are invisible when worn.

But don't be fooled by their size. They're so powerful, they can do virtually all the clever things our ears are designed for - giving you the immersive, sensory experience of hearing again.

*continued overleaf...*

 ASSURED HEARING CARE     INVESTORS IN PEOPLE | Silver

----

### For appointments please call
### FREE on 0800 4370 045
or complete and return this coupon

Please make sure we have your correct telephone number as we need to call to confirm your appointment

### YES PLEASE arrange a FREE
### Hidden Hearing assessment

☐ at my preferred Hidden Hearing centre    ☐ at home

I currently wear a hearing aid:   ☐ Yes ☐ No

**Your Contact Details:**

Tel:

Mobile:

Email:

*Hidden Hearing - A strong visual letter with the added punch of a coupon*

## Take a FREE hearing test this month

Maybe you need a hearing aid, maybe you don't. We simply don't know. So the experts at your local Hidden Hearing Centre will spend an hour with you, finding out. They'll talk to you about your lifestyle and the type of problems you've had...then after an audiometric test (that's completely painless), they'll give you all the answers you need. And help you decide what to do next.

If they find that your hearing is fine, they will tell you so. Just as any reputable optician would never sell a pair of specs to fix 20-20 vision, Hidden Hearing will never sell anyone a hearing aid without reason. In fact, if your hearing is fine, they'll tell you how to look after it - so that you continue to hear well for as long as nature allows.

On the other hand, of course, if your test shows that your hearing could be improved, you'll have all the help - and time - you need to choose a new hearing aid that fits with your budget and lifestyle. Either way, there's no charge for your test - and no obligation whatsoever.

**To take a free hearing test, and get the answers you need, call your local Hearing Centre on FREEPHONE 0800 4370 045 today**

Hidden Hearing makes a point of keeping waiting lists short, so you can probably take your test in the next 7 days. Then by the next time you get together with the people you love, you'll have plenty to talk about... and no problem joining in.

Wishing you a lifetime of better hearing.

Yours sincerely

Graham Lane
Managing Director

**P.S. Please don't delay - call 0800 4370 045 to arrange your appointment now. Then if you choose a new hearing aid, you'll have it custom-made and fitted in just a few weeks.**

**Book your FREE hearing test this month and your name will be entered into a prize draw to win a £250 Marks & Spencer Voucher**

**Hidden Hearing Limited** Medway Street, Maidstone, Kent ME14 1HL
REGISTERED IN ENGLAND & WALES No. 1990227   www.hiddenhearing.co.uk

Hidden Hearing is committed to protecting your personal data in compliance with the Data Protection Act 1998. No personal data will be passed on to any third party.

☐ Your telephone number will be used to confirm your appointment. All telephone calls may be recorded for training purposes. If you are NOT happy for us to contact you by phone for future communications, please tick the box

By completing your email address you are agreeing to receive information on Hidden Hearing electronically. Should you not wish to receive information in this manner, please leave the email box blank

☐ Your address details will only be used to keep you up-to-date with our products, services and offers. Should you NOT wish us to use your postal address for this purpose please tick the box.

*VK Direct - Dustin The Dustmite - A follow-up, for people who ignored a vacuum cleaner promotion*

Delivered by

Royal Mail

ROYAL MAIL

POSTAGE PAID GB
HQ 6698

**Title; FName; SName**
**Addressline_1**
**Addressline_2**
**Town**
**County**
**POSTCODE**

*VK Direct - Dustin The Dustmite - A follow-up, for people who ignored a vacuum cleaner promotion*

# Yo!

Me and the boys

It's a quick note to say big, BIG thanks for not buying that Vorwerk cleaner thing! Me and the lads are lovin' it massiv down here in the shagpile, and we don't want no supervac messin' it up for us, yeah?

Let me tell you,

## THAT THING IS A KILLER!

I'd say ask my cousin Denzil, but you can't cos he got sucked!

### What happened to Denzil
### (you might find this distressin')

He was a good dustmite. Alright, he munched people's skin for a living and he might have caused an asthma attak now and then, but we all do that, don't we? (I do - it's wicked)

Anyways, he was hanging about a few streets away, minding his own and totally lovin' their old cylinder vac! Like every time that nozzle hit the carpet, Denzil and his gang was like "Whatever!" and "Come and have a go dude! NOT!"

Reconstruction

### THEN TRAGEDY STRUCK
### (the nasty bit)

The humans only went and bought a Vorwerk! Serious - no warning, nothin! One minute, D and the crew is ravin' in the upholstery, next it's goodnight and right up the scary nozzly bit to oblivion!

# Man, I am so glad you ain't bought that thing!

Here's 5 reasons why **YOU MUST NEVER GET A VORWERK** no matter what:

1. **It's ruthless!** Every other vac I've seen leaves us well alone. This babe don't give us no chance! ZERO!!

2. **It gets everywhere!** It's got bendy attachments, a low head to get under the sofa..**it cuts off our food supply,** and blasts us out of the secret hidey-hole. (EVIL!!)

3. **It dry cleans!** There's like this powder. As if suckin' us ain't good enough, now they're totally stickin' the boot in!

4. **IT'S GOT A MATTRESS EVICTION THING!** Listen, my mate Clive is upstairs **RIGHT NOW**, chomping his way through flaky skin bits – and let me tell you **he does not** want this gig to end!!

5. **It lasts for ages!** Most vacs need replacin' like every 3 or 4 years, and even then they ain't much use! This monster lives for **decades!** You'd be wipin' out a whole generation!

# So, like I said – thanks, innit!

I probably owe you a favour or summin', but you ain't gettin' it cos I'm just in it for me, yeah? (That's why they call me a parasite) **Ha ha ha!!**

Thanks again - love 'n night-bites

# Dustin

**Dustin T. Dustmite (Esq)**

PS. Say hi to Clive later.
And IF YOU SEE THIS OFFER OFF VORWERK, DO NOT CALL. DO NOT EMAIL... Look the other way or summin! Sorted.

*VK Direct - Dustin The Dustmite - A follow-up, for people who ignored a vacuum cleaner promotion*

## Before You Mail Another Letter - Put Your Campaign Under The Microscope

# Apply for a FREE 1-2-1 Campaign Review with David Amor & James Daniel...and Discover At Least 7 Ways to Increase ROI

### *Limited Availability – Apply NOW*

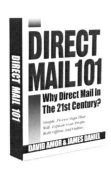

You've got the manual – all good so far. But how do you make the leap, from generic best practice that works in any business...to actionable strategies that work in a business likes yours?

How do you break your mailing list into segments? Plan for long-term profits? Create irresistible offers? Grab attention with headlines? Test and measure?

There's so much to do, so much to master, that it's easy to fall behind.

**So submit your campaign to David and James, and apply for a 40 minute review call.** If accepted, the two authors will assess your whole campaign, from list to letter. You'll get specific action points that will slash your mailing costs and multiply response rates. Free of charge, with no obligation.

### To qualify for this exclusive limited offer, you must be:

- ✓ **The owner of your business, or a senior decision maker**
- ✓ Planning a full-scale campaign, to 20,000 prospects or more
- ✓ **Ready to go, with a brand new campaign – or one you've already tested**
- ✓ Committed to testing, measuring and optimising your mailer
- ✓ **Ready...and able...to scale up, and make 7 figures plus**
- ✓ Happy to share your experience of working with David & James

### Ready? Upload Your Letter and Campaign Plans to

# MyDMCampaign.com

Offer subject to qualification and availability. For terms & conditions see website

## NOTES

Upload campaign to My DMCampaign.com
as soon as possible!

# NOTES

# NOTES

# NOTES

# NOTES

# NOTES

# NOTES

# NOTES

# NOTES

# NOTES

# NOTES

# NOTES

# NOTES